CULTURES OF THE WORLD

ALGERIA

Falaq Kagda

MARSHALL CAVENDISH
New York • London • Sydney

Reference edition reprinted 2000 by
Marshall Cavendish Corporation
99 White Plains Road
Tarrytown
New York 10591

© Times Media Private Limited 1997

Originated and designed by
Times Books International, an imprint of
Times Media Private Limited, a member of the
Times Publishing Group

Printed in Singapore

Library of Congress Cataloging-in-Publication Data:
Kagda, Falaq.
    Algeria / Falaq Kagda.
      p. cm. — (Cultures of the world)
    Includes bibliographical references (p.) and index.
    Summary: Examines the geography, history, government,
economy, people, and culture of Algeria.
    ISBN 0-7614-0680-8 (library binding)
     1. Algeria—Juvenile literature. [1. Algeria.]
I. Title. II. Series.
DK93.K34 1997
965—dc21   96-40373
              CIP
              AC

INTRODUCTION

ALGERIA FORMS PART OF the region that its early Arab conquerors called the "Island of the West" *(Jazirat al Maghrib)*—the land between the "Sea of Sand" (the Sahara) and the Mediterranean Sea. Algerians share a common language, religion, and cultural heritage with their Maghribi neighbors and, in large measure, a common history as well. Like other countries of North Africa, Algeria's population is divided between the original Berber inhabitants and the Arab conquerors who settled there in the seventh century.

During the 132 years of French rule, the country's traditional lifestyle underwent massive changes as the culture was subjected to French domination. Since the brutal eight-year "war of liberation" ended in 1962, Algeria has been an independent nation determined to forge once again a common identity for its mixed population. The principal unifying force in this search for a national identity has been Islam, shared by the great majority of Algerians.

CONTENTS

A shop sells handicrafts.

CONTENTS

An old man from an Algerian village.

GEOGRAPHY

THE DEMOCRATIC AND POPULAR REPUBLIC OF ALGERIA, in northwest Africa, is part of the Maghrib ("MAH-grib"), a region in North Africa between the Mediterranean Sea and the Sahara. The Maghrib includes the Atlas Mountains and the coastal plain of northwest Africa. The name— Arabic for "west"—generally refers to Morocco, Algeria, Tunisia, and sometimes Libya. Spain was included at the time of Moorish domination (8th to 15th centuries).

Algeria is Africa's second largest country, after Sudan. Algeria has many neighbors: Tunisia lies to the northeast, Libya to the east, Niger and Mali to the south, and Mauritania, Morocco, and Western Sahara to the west and northwest. The Mediterranean Sea defines Algeria's northern border. Algeria's position at the crossroads of Europe, Africa, and the Middle East has given it a prominent position in world affairs.

Opposite: **A Tuareg walking in the Sahara. Hot, dry desert covers more than 80 percent of Algeria.**

Left: **The desert has many different looks, such as the lunar landscape of the Tassili Plateau.**

TOPOGRAPHY

Topographically, Algeria consists of a series of contrasting, approximately parallel east-west zones. The narrow alluvial plains along the coast—the most fertile land in Algeria—are separated from the Sahara by the ranges and plateaux of the Atlas Mountains. The Tell Atlas, which reaches heights of more than 7,550 feet (2,300 m), includes the Hodna range and the spectacular Djurdjura Massif of Kabylia in northeastern Algeria.

A semiarid plateau with an average elevation of 2,800 feet (850 m) separates the Tell Atlas from the Saharan Atlas. In the east, the plateau merges with the Aurès Mountains, which boast Mount Chelia (7,648 feet/2,330 m), the highest peak in northern Algeria. South of the Saharan Atlas is the immense Sahara Desert, with its gravel expanses, plateaux, sand dunes (*ergs* in Arabic, pronounced "ehrgs") and the fascinating lunarlike Ahaggar Massif, where Mount Tahat, the nation's highest peak, rises to 9,852 feet (3,001 m).

The eastern part of the coast is more rugged than the gently rolling slopes of the western Tell.

THE TELL REGION Most Algerian cities and 90 percent of the population inhabit the fertile coastal area called the Tell (which means "hill" in Arabic). The country's best farmland, the Tell was named for its rolling hills and valleys. Most of Algeria's rivers are here, keeping the land fertile. The rivers flood during the rainy season and drain into the Mediterranean. In the summer, they often slow to a trickle, and dry riverbeds are a common sight.

THE HIGH PLATEAU REGION Separating the Tell and Saharan mountains, this region rises 1,300–4,300 feet (400–1,300 m) above sea level.

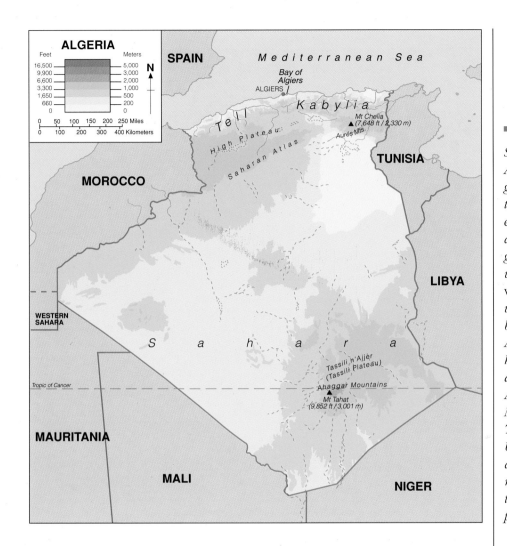

ALGERIA

Feet		Meters
16,500		5,000
9,900		3,000
6,600		2,000
3,300		1,000
1,650		500
660		200
0		0

0 50 100 150 200 250 Miles
0 100 200 300 400 Kilometers

N

SPAIN

M e d i t e r r a n e a n   S e a

Bay of Algiers

ALGIERS

K a b y l i a

T e l l

High Plateau

Mt Chelia
▲ (7,648 ft / 2,330 m)

Aurés Mts.

Saharan Atlas

TUNISIA

MOROCCO

LIBYA

WESTERN SAHARA

S a h a r a

Tassili n'Ajjer
(Tassili Plateau)

Ahaggar Mountains

Tropic of Cancer

Mt Tahat
▲ (9,852 ft / 3,001 m)

MAURITANIA

MALI

NIGER

Since 1975, the Algerian government has tried to curb the encroaching desert. The grandest project *was the* barrage vert *["BAH-rahge vair"], or green barrier. Rows of Aleppo pine trees have been planted along the Saharan Atlas ridge from Morocco to the Tunisian border. Unfortunately, the desert creeps northward quicker than workers can plant trees.*

Much of it is rocky and dry. Cattle, sheep, and goats graze on small clumps of vegetation, shrubs, scrub pines, oak trees, and wild esparto grass dotting the plateau and grassland leading into the Saharan Atlas Mountains. Only about 7 percent of Algerians live here, mostly herders. Some are nomads who go from pasture to pasture to feed their flocks on the grasses and shrubs that cover most of the area.

For three to five weeks each summer, the sirocco sweeps the plateaux. This powerful, dusty, hot wind whips northward from the Sahara, blowing sand as far as the coastal Tell.

THE WORLD'S LARGEST DESERT

The Sahara is the largest desert in the world. Spanning the continent from the Atlantic Ocean to the Red Sea, it extends north from the Niger River and Lake Chad to the Atlas Mountains and the Mediterranean Sea. The name Sahara is from the Arabic word for desert. The grasslands of West Africa, which form the Sahara's southern boundary, are called the Sahel. The Sahara covers about 3,300,000 square miles (8,547,000 square km). Morocco, Algeria, Tunisia, Mali, Niger, Chad, and Sudan have large desert regions. Most of Libya, Egypt, and Mauritania are located in the Sahara.

The folded rocks of the Saharan Atlas Mountains delineate the northern boundary of the Algerian Sahara. Once these mountains supported extensive Atlas cedar forests, but most trees were harvested for fuel and building supplies. Now the denuded mountains serve mainly as a gateway to the world's largest desert. To the south, the Sahara dashes the image many have of deserts as an endless expanse of golden sand. The sand gives way to plateaux of black pebbles. These in turn change into wide expanses of red sand. Farther southeast are large sandstone rock formations, which signal the beginning of the Ahaggar Mountains. Here towers Mount Tahat, sometimes with snow on its peak.

Oases are the only areas of greenery in the Sahara, and look unusually built up in the midst of the arid desert. Date palms, which sustain the desert economy, surround these communities (shown above). Shown opposite is an oasis town that has been buried by encroaching desert. About 3 percent of Algerians live in the desert. Most settle on oases and grow dates and citrus fruits. Fewer are nomads, who travel from pasture to pasture with their camels and other livestock. More recently, the northeastern Sahara has sprouted derricks and rigs pumping out the oil and natural gas that lie beneath the desert.

The northern Sahara gets about four to eight inches (10–20 cm) of rainfall a year in winter. Things are a little better during summer, when wet monsoon winds from the Gulf of Guinea penetrate inland to the Sahel, bringing 10–20 inches (25–50 cm) of rainfall annually. Most of the

Sahara, however, receives less than 5 inches (13 cm) of rainfall annually, and large areas experience no rainfall for years at a time.

The Sahara is also very hot. The average annual temperature is 80°F (27°C). Because of high temperatures and clear skies, humidity can be as low as 2.5 percent, the lowest in the world. Parts of the Sahara experience 50 to 75 days per year of wind and blowing sand. Although the climate has remained relatively uniform, extended periods of drought are common. The Sahel drought of 1968–1974 is the most recent.

The Sahara has an extensive network of dry streambeds, or *wadi* ("WAH-dee"), that were formed during earlier wet periods. Many streams appear in the wadis after rainfall, flowing from the Atlas Mountains and central Saharan uplands into surrounding basins, where occasional salt marshes, called *sebkhas*, are found. Underground water, or oases, that can support irrigated agriculture are found in many wadis and depressions.

The sands of the Sahara hide a wealth of mineral resources. It has substantial crude petroleum reserves. Libya and Algeria are the largest oil producers, and Algeria is also an important producer and exporter of natural gas. Algeria also has iron ore deposits and manganese, and numerous metals are found in the central Saharan uplands.

The traditional camel caravans that used to traverse the deserts—an image popularized by movies such as *Lawrence of Arabia*—have today been replaced by truck convoys over the same routes. The Saharan road system is steadily expanding, although only two main routes cross the desert from central Algeria to Nigeria and to southern Mali. The best road and rail transportation is associated with mineral exploitation. Many international air routes cross the Sahara.

Springtime comes to the Algerian coast near the border with Morocco.

CLIMATE AND DRAINAGE

Algerian weather varies according to geography. In the Tell, the Mediterranean keeps the climate mild, with temperatures averaging a balmy 77°F (25°C) in summer and 52°F (11°C) in winter. Rainfall is abundant along the coast, although less rain falls in the west (15 inches/38 cm annually in Oran) than in the east (26 inches/66 cm annually in Algiers). The Tell Atlas is also much drier in the west than it is in Kabylia, which receives only about 40 inches (102 cm) of rainfall a year. Snow on the Djurdjura Massif also supplies water when it melts in spring. The Cheliff in the coastal plain, the only significant stream, is unnavigable, but provides water for irrigation.

In the ranges and plateaux of the Atlas Mountains, temperatures are harsher, ranging from 39°F (4°C) to 82°F (28°C). Rainfall is limited in the High Plateau region, but during the rainy season streams drain into the shallow salt marshes called *shatts*.

In the desert, underground rivers offer the only water. The practically rainless Sahara receives less than 5 inches (13 cm) of rainfall a year. A small part of the desert crosses the Tropic of Cancer, where temperatures are blistering even in winter. Daytime temperatures have climbed to an unforgiving 122°F (50°C) in the midday sun. However, the dryness allows the air to cool quickly once the sun disappears. Evening temperatures can drop quickly and seem freezing after the scorching daytime heat. Extreme daily temperature variations are common when the harsh sirocco winds blow in from the desert.

BARBARY APE

The Barbary ape, so called since ancient times, is actually a monkey, not an ape. It is a macaque, *Macaca sylvana*. The Barbary ape is 15–30 inches (38–76 cm) long and weighs up to 28 pounds (13 kg). Its life span in captivity is more than 30 years. With thick yellowish brown to black fur and hairless, whitish pink faces, Barbary apes are the only wild monkeys now living in Europe. They occupy caves on the Rock of Gibraltar and in the rocky areas of Morocco and Algeria. It is thought that they may have been taken westward during the Arab expansion of the Middle Ages. According to legend, British dominion will end when the Barbary ape is gone from the British-held Rock of Gibraltar.

FLORA AND FAUNA

Although once quite densely foliated for a country that is 80 percent desert, Algeria today is much denuded of its greenery. In the Tell, just west of Algiers, lie citrus groves and vineyards. Fig trees and indigenous olive trees flourish along the coast. Aleppo pine, juniper, and cork trees grow on the rugged mountain slopes of the Kabylia and Aurès along the eastern coast and southern part of the region.

Vegetation in the semiarid areas includes drinn and esparto grass. Few areas of the desert are completely lacking in vegetation. A minimal cover of xerophytic shrubs (shrubs adapted to hot, dry climates) extends to the northern edge of the desert; coarse grasses grow in depressions; and acacia trees and date palms grow in valleys and oases. Thorn woodlands and wooded grasslands are found in the Sahel. Some animal life exists even in the desert's interior: insects, small rodents, reptiles, and on the plateaux, gazelles.

Although the harsh environment limits wildlife, there are boars, antelopes, jackals, hares, several endangered Barbary species (ape, red deer, hyena, leopard), and scorpions and insects. And, of course, camels are plentiful.

THE CAMEL

Domesticated thousands of years ago by frankincense traders, who trained the gangly cud-chewer to make the long and arduous journey from southern Arabia to the northern regions of the Middle East, the camel went on to become the desert dweller's primary source of transport, shade, milk, meat, wool, and hides. But in technologically advanced Saudi Arabia, even the Bedouin are not as dependent on the camel as they once were. These days, camels are valued more as thoroughbred racing animals and sentimental images of the past than as the mainstay of transportation, but in many parts of Africa and Asia today, camels still pull plows, turn waterwheels, and transport people and goods to market along desert routes impassable by wheeled vehicles.

Here's an introduction to the special characteristics, body structure, and behavior patterns of this amazing creature.

ATA ALLAH, GOD'S GIFT The Bedouin name for *Camelus dromedarius*, the one-hump dromedary, also known as the Arabian camel.

BEHAVIOR Unpredictable at best. Camels have the reputation of being bad-tempered and obstinate creatures who spit and kick. In reality, they tend to be good-tempered, patient, and intelligent. The moaning and bawling sound they make when they're loaded up and have to rise to their feet is like the grunting and heavy breathing of a weight lifter in action, not a sign of displeasure at having to do some work.

BODY TEMPERATURE Camels do not pant, and they perspire very little. Humans start to sweat when the outside temperature rises above the normal body temperature of 98.6°F (37°C), but the camel has a unique body thermostat. It can raise its body temperature tolerance level as much as 11°F (6°C) before perspiring, thereby conserving body fluids and avoiding unnecessary water loss. No other mammal can do this. Because the camel's body temperature is often lower than air temperature, a group of resting camels will avoid excessive heat by pressing against each other.

EARS A camel's hearing is acute—even if it chooses to pay no attention when given a command! A camel's ears are lined with fur to filter out sand and dust blowing into the ear canal.

EYES A camel's eyes are large, with a soft, doe-like expression. They are protected by a double row of long curly eyelashes that also help keep out sand and dust, while thick bushy eyebrows shield the eyes from the desert sun.

FEET Camels have broad, flat, leathery pads with two toes on each foot. When the camel places its foot down, the pads spread, preventing the foot from sinking into the sand. When walking, the camel moves both feet on one side of its body, then both feet on the other. This gait suggests the rolling motion of a boat, explaining the camel's "ship of the desert" nickname.

FOOD A camel can go 5–7 days with little or no food and water, and can lose a quarter of its body weight without impairing its normal functions. Domesticated camels rely on man for their preferred food of dates, grass, and grains such as wheat and oats, but a camel can survive on thorny scrub or whatever it can find—bones, seeds, dried leaves, or even its owner's tent.

HAIR Camels come in every shade of brown, from cream to almost black. All camels moult in spring and grow a new coat by autumn. Camel hair is sought after worldwide for high-quality coats, garments, and artists' brushes, as well as being used to make traditional Bedouin rugs and tents. A camel can shed as much as 5 pounds (2 kg) of hair at each moult.

HUMP Contrary to popular belief, a camel does not store water in its hump. The hump is a mound of fatty tissue from which the animal draws energy when food is hard to find. When a camel uses its hump fat for sustenance, the mound becomes flabby and shrinks. If a camel draws too much fat, the small remaining lump will flop from its upright position and hang down the camel's side. Food and a few days' rest will return the hump to its normal firm condition.

LIFE SPAN After a gestation period of 13 months, a camel cow usually bears a single calf, occasionally twins. Calves walk within hours of birth, but remain close to their mothers until they reach maturity at five years of age. The normal life span of a camel is 40 years, although a working camel retires from active duty at 25.

WATER Although camels can withstand severe dehydration, a large animal can drink as much as 26 gallons (100 l) in 10 minutes. Such an amount would kill another mammal, but the camel's unique metabolism enables the animal to store the water in its bloodstream.

ALGIERS

Algiers is Algeria's oldest, largest, and most historic city. Phoenicians settled here approximately 3,000 years ago. For almost 500 years Algiers was a colonial capital under Turkish and French rule before becoming the national capital after independence. With a population of 1.5 million (1987), Algiers (in French, Alger; in Arabic, al-Jazair) is Algeria's largest city and chief port.

Algiers was known to the Romans as Icosium. After being razed several times by invaders, the present site was settled in the 10th century by the Berbers. Until the 18th century, Algiers was a home base for Barbary pirates, who terrorized ships on the Mediterranean. In 1516, Algiers came under Turkish control. The French captured the city in 1830, and it became the colonial headquarters of France until Algeria's independence in 1962. During World War II, Algiers served as a major headquarters for the Allies, and for a brief period was the provisional capital of free France.

Algiers is built on a hillside, where European-style buildings surround an old Muslim town overlooking Mediterranean waters. To the west, the Sahel Hills cut Algiers off from surrounding farmlands. Flowers and palm trees line the main road leading to the city center, where a memorial to African culture stands. History lives in the Prehistory and Ethnographic Museum that was once the Turkish Bardo Palace. Historic buildings blend gracefully with classic Turkish and Islamic architecture in the midst of modern high-rises and businesses. Algiers is the site of the University of Algiers (established in 1879). Notable buildings include the Great Mosque (built in the 11th century) and the national library.

The old Turkish harbor is Algeria's busiest port and the mainstay of the economy. Fishing boats, yachts, and the Algerian navy share the waters with vessels carrying products from the surrounding agricultural region, such as oil, wine, fruit, and vegetable exports. Iron ore is also exported, and the harbor serves as a refueling depot for large vessels. Turn-of-the-century buildings line the semicircular bay and lead to the business district immediately behind. Cement, chemicals, and paper products are manufactured in the city.

The most colorful part of the city is the famous Casbah. *Casbah* ("KAHZ-bah") is Arabic for Turkish fortress. After independence, the government wanted to move residents to new housing and proclaim the Casbah a historic district, but Algerians protested and the government capitulated. The area is alive with children playing in front of dilapidated homes. Narrow streets lead to the *souk* ("sook") or market, with stalls of crafts, fruits, vegetables, and freshly slaughtered sheep hung in rows.

A narrow street in the Casbah. During French rule, native Algerians were segregated into this section. The Casbah was the center of anti-French activity throughout the Algerian revolution.

ORAN

About 225 miles (360 km) west of Algiers, along the coast between Algiers and the Moroccan border, lies Oran (Wahran in Arabic). Oran sits on high cliff plateaux that plunge into the Mediterranean. The city's long history is reflected in its old Spanish fortress, its mosque, its French-built port facilities and Nouvelle Ville (New City), and the recently founded Université d'Oran (established 1965).

Oran is Algeria's second-largest city and the one most dominated by European influence. First built as a breakwater by Arabs from Spain in 903, the city later became a prosperous port under the Almohads and under Spanish occupation from the 16th to 18th centuries. The French designed Oran as Algeria's major second city, which had, until recently, more cathedrals than mosques.

Oran has a frontage road lined with palm trees along the Mediterranean. Elegant French houses mix with modern office and apartment buildings overlooking an imposing bay and busy harbor.

CONSTANTINE

Constantine (ancient Cirta) is the capital of Constantine province in northeast Algeria. Algeria's third largest city, Constantine is central to many of the most outstanding Roman ruins in the world. The straight streets, wide squares, and administrative buildings of the city's northwest sector speak of its Roman and French heritage. The Arab sector in the southeast is characterized by winding streets and craft markets.

Located 50 miles (80 km) inland near the Tunisian border, Constantine stretches over the top of a huge chalk cliff and is dramatically cut off from the surrounding plateau on three sides by the Rhumel River gorge.

Probably settled in prehistoric times, Constantine was the prosperous capital of Numidia under the powerful Numidian King Massinissa by the third century B.C. In A.D. 313 the city was renamed for the Roman Emperor Constantine I, who rebuilt the city after it was destroyed in the war preceding his accession. Frequently contested by various Muslim dynasties, Constantine fell to the Turks in the 16th century and to the French in 1837.

Constantine is built on the top of high cliffs.

HISTORY

THE INHABITANTS OF THE COASTAL AREA of present-day Algeria shared in an early Neolithic culture that was common to the whole Mediterranean littoral before the 15th century B.C. South of the Atlas Mountains, nomadic hunters and herders roamed the vast savanna, abounding in game, that 8,000 years ago stretched across what is now the Sahara. The savanna people scattered south and east into the Sudan region before the encroaching desert and invading horsemen. Others may have migrated northward, where they were eventually absorbed by the Berbers.

The origin of the Berbers is a mystery. Research has produced an abundance of educated speculation without any definitive solution. Linguistic evidence suggests southwestern Asia as the point from which the ancestors of the Berbers began their migration into North Africa early in the third millennium B.C.

French paleontologist Camille Arambourg discovered the skeletal and cultural remains of Ternifine man on the Agris Plain near Oran, in 1954–1955.

Opposite: **The early savanna people left a vivid picture of their image of the world in graceful rock paintings like those found at Tassili n'Ajjer.**

Left: **Ruins at Carthage. Carthage, essentially a maritime power, hired Berber mercenaries for its overseas military expeditions, but the emerging power of Rome contested Carthaginian expansion in the western Mediterranean.**

TASSILI N'AJJER

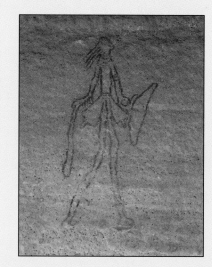

Tassili n'Ajjer ("tah-see-LEE nahd-JAIR"), a plateau in the Saharan area of southern Algeria, is where French archeologist Henri Lhote discovered a large group of prehistoric rock paintings in 1956–1957. The paintings in Tassili n'Ajjer's rock shelters and caves date from the fourth to third millennia B.C., a time when hunter-gatherers and pastoralists flourished in a Sahara that enjoyed a much higher level of rainfall.

Painted over a period of 4,000 years, they are the most complete existing record of a prehistoric African culture and among the most remarkable Stone Age remains to be found anywhere. In a wide variety of styles ranging from naturalistic to abstract, the rock paintings depict the wild Saharan fauna and herds of domestic cattle and sheep. The inhabitants of the cave used a distinctive type of pottery known as Dotted Wavy Line, as well as ground and polished stone axes and adzes. They cultivated cereal crops but relied for much of their diet on hunting, gathering, and fishing in shallow lakes. The culture depicted in the rock paintings flourished until the region began to dry up as a result of climatic changes after 4000 B.C., but the prehistoric savanna has been described as the nursery for subsequent African civilization. The Tassili art is important for the light it throws on prehistoric migrations and economic practices in the Saharan savanna.

CARTHAGE

Minoan seamen from Crete may have set up depots on the coast of present-day Algeria before 2000 B.C., but it was only with the arrival of Phoenician traders, who penetrated the western Mediterranean before the 12th century B.C., that the region entered into recorded history. Eventually, Punic trading posts were established along the African coast, where the merchants of Tyre and, later, Carthage developed commercial relations with the Berber tribes of the interior and paid them tribute to ensure their cooperation in the exploitation of raw materials.

By the fifth century B.C. Carthage, the greatest of the overseas Punic colonies, had extended its hegemony across much of North Africa. Defeated in the long Punic wars (third century B.C.), Carthage was reduced by Rome to the status of a small and vulnerable African state at the mercy of the Berber tribes, but its influence on North Africa remained deep.

BERBER KINGDOMS

The basic unit of social and political organization among the Berbers was the extended family, usually identified with a particular village or traditional grazing grounds. Families in turn were bound together in the clan. An alliance of clans, often tracing their origins to a common ancestor as a symbol of unity, formed a tribe. For mutual defense kindred tribes joined in confederations which, because war was a permanent feature of tribal life, were in time institutionalized. Some chieftains, successful in battle, established rudimentary territorial states; but their kingdoms were easily fragmented, and dynasties rarely survived a generation. By the second century B.C., however, several large but loosely administered Berber kingdoms had emerged. Two kingdoms were established in Numidia, behind the coastal areas controlled by Carthage.

One of the most illustrious of the Berber monarchs was Massinissa (*c.* 240–148 B.C.), who had served with the Carthaginians in Spain. Massinissa shifted his support to Rome to be counted among the victor's allies when Carthage surrendered in 202 B.C. He united Numidia and extended his authority from the Moulouya to Cyrenaica, a territory that he governed from his court of Cirta (Constantine). Numidia was divided among several heirs after Massinissa's death. Rome intervened when his grandson, Jugurtha (118–105 B.C.), attempted to reunite the Berber kingdoms. Betrayed by a rival chieftain at the end of a long war in which he pinned down large numbers of Roman troops, Jugurtha was taken to Rome and starved to death in the Capitol.

Jugurtha betrayed to the Roman commander by a rival chieftain.

TIMGAD

The ruins of Timgad (ancient Thamugadi), in northeastern Algeria about 220 miles (350 km) southeast of Algiers, are the most complete of all the Roman centers in North Africa. Excavation begun by a French team in 1881 laid bare the entire plan of the colony. Founded in A.D. 100 by Emperor Trajan as a settlement for army veterans, Thamugadi was sited in rich farmland. The settlement prospered through commerce and agriculture; by A.D. 150 it had grown beyond its walls into the surrounding countryside. Saharan raiders sacked it in the fifth century.

The site's plan resembles a military camp but was designed for civilian occupation. The walls enclose a square area, 1,165 feet (355 m) per side, divided into quadrants by two colonnaded avenues and subdivided by a grid of streets. The crowding of temples, baths, markets, offices, a theater, and houses within the walls forced many of the larger structures, especially baths, outside. Almost no sculpture has been preserved, but the remains of mosaic floors are notable.

There are many Roman ruins still in Algeria, such as these at Guelma in northeast Algeria.

ROMAN NORTH AFRICA

The royal house of Massinissa ruled Numidia as a Roman protectorate until Julius Caesar deposed its king and attached a part of it to Proconsular Africa (present-day Tunisia), which had become a Roman province in 146 B.C. Sovereignty over the rest was transferred to Mauritania, where Massinissa's line survived until A.D. 24, when the satellite kingdom was also annexed to the Roman empire.

Rome sought to control only those areas that were economically useful or could be defended easily. Called the "granary of the empire," the North African provinces were valued for their agricultural exports, Italy's main source of food. On vast imperial estates acquired by the Roman aristocracy, land was rented to Berber tenants who paid taxes and rent with grain that went to feed the army and provide free bread for the dole in Rome.

The Vandals, a Germanic tribe, crossed from Spain in 429, seized power, and established a kingdom. Although Rome eventually recognized their overlordship in North Africa, the Vandals confined their rule to the most economically profitable areas. There they constituted an isolated warrior caste. Civil administration was left in Roman hands.

ISLAM AND THE ARABS

The most significant influence on Berber culture was the result of the Arab invasion of the 7th and 11th centuries. By the time of his death in 632 Prophet Mohammed and his followers had brought most of the tribes and towns of the Arabian Peninsula under the banner of Islam. Within a generation Arab armies had carried Islam westward across North Africa as far as Tripolitania. There stiff Berber resistance slowed the Arab advance, and efforts at permanent conquest were resumed only when it became apparent that the Maghrib could be opened up as a theater of operations in the Muslim campaign against the Byzantine empire.

In 670, the Arabs surged into the Roman province of Africa, where they founded the city of Al Qayrawan 100 miles (160 km) south of Carthage. Pushed back on their own resources, the Berber farmers of Numidia looked once again to the tribal chieftains for leadership. For a time the Arab advance was halted and Al Qayrawan put on the defensive, but by the end of the century fresh Arab troops, reinforced by newly converted Muslim Berber auxiliaries, had subdued the Numidian countryside. The last pockets of Byzantine resistance on the North African coast were wiped out only after the Arabs had obtained naval supremacy in the Mediterranean.

Sedentary Berber tribespeople turned now to the Arabs for protection against their nomadic kin. They differed essentially from the Arabs in their political culture, however, and their communal and representative institutions contrasted sharply with the personal and authoritarian government of the Arabs. Even after their conversion to Islam, Berber tribes retained their customary laws in preference to Islamic law.

The Arabs formed an urban elite in the Maghrib, where they had come as conquerors and missionaries, not as colonists. Their armies traveled without women and married among the sedentary Berbers, transmitting

Muslim Spain and the Maghrib, which had been conquered within 50 years of the founding of Al Qayrawan, were organized under the political and religious leadership of the Umayyad caliph of Damascus.

25

An Arab warrior on his camel leads an attack.

Arab culture and Islam to the townspeople and farmers. But conversion to Islam was more rapid among the nomadic tribes of the hinterland, who stoutly resisted Arab political domination. The Berbers, with their characteristic love of independence and impassioned religious temperament, shaped Islam in their own image. They embraced schismatic Muslim sects—often traditional folk religion barely disguised as Islam—as a way of breaking from Arab control.

The heretical Kharidjite movement surfaced in Morocco as a revolt against the Arabs in 739. The Berber Kharidjites ("seceders;" from the Arabic *khurudj*, meaning abandon) proclaimed that any suitable Muslim candidate could be elected caliph without regard to his race, station, or descent from the Prophet. The attack on Arab monopoly of the religious leadership of Islam was explicit in Kharidjite doctrine, and Berbers across the Maghrib rose in revolt in the name of religion against Arab domination. In the wake of the revolt, Kharidjite sectarians established a number of theocratic tribal kingdoms, most of which had short histories.

One of these kingdoms, the Rustumid dynasty, extended its rule over most of the central Maghrib. The Rustumids gained a reputation throughout the Islamic world for honesty and justice, as well as for the openness and egalitarian nature of their imams. The court at Tahert (present-day Tiaret) was noted for its patronage of learning in mathematics, astronomy, and astrology, as well as theology and law, but the Rustumid imams failed, by choice or by neglect, to organize a reliable standing army. This important factor, accompanied by the dynasty's eventual lapse into decadence, opened the way for Tahert's demise under the assault of the Fatimids.

FATIMIDS

In the closing decade of the ninth century, missionaries of the Ismaili sect of Shi'a Islam converted the Kutama Berbers of the Kabylia region and led them on a crusade against the Sunni rulers of Ifriquiya. Al Qayrawan fell to them in 909, and the next year the Kutama installed the Ismaili grand master from Syria as imam of their movement and ruler over their territory. The imam initiated the Fatimid dynasty, named after Fatima, daughter of Mohammed, from whom he claimed descent.

The Fatimids turned westward in 911, destroying the Kharidjite imamate at Tahert and claiming the central Maghrib for Shi'ism. Kharidjite refugees fled south into the desert. They settled in the M'zab Valley.

For many years the Fatimids posed a threat to Morocco, but eventually they turned their attention eastward. By 969, they had completed the conquest of Egypt and moved their capital to the new city that they founded at Cairo, where they established a Shi'a caliphate.

ALMORAVIDS

The Almoravids ruled North Africa and Spain from 1056 to 1147. The dynasty originated in the western Sahara among the Berbers. From the mouth of the Senegal River, warriors spread a simple, fundamentalist form of Islam; they moved northward into Morocco and conquered North Africa as far as Algiers. Marrakesh was founded as the capital about 1070.

In 1086, the Almoravids crossed into Spain, defeated the Christian army of reconquest, and annexed the territories of Muslim Spain. These rugged Berber nomads were conquered in turn by the refined civilization of Spain and were unable to defend their empire against the Almohads, another Berber dynasty, who killed the last Almoravid ruler in 1147.

Fleeing Kharidjites settled in oases in the M'zab region, where they founded cities where their descendants remain today.

ALMOHADS

The Almohads ruled North Africa and Spain from 1130 to 1269. The dynasty originated in a mass movement initially led by Ibn Tumart, who proclaimed himself the Mahdi, or messiah, come to purify Islam. His successor, Abd al-Mumin, defeated the Almoravids and made Marrakesh the capital in 1147. Subsequently, all the Muslim territory in Spain was occupied, and North Africa was conquered as far as Tripoli by 1160.

The Almohad court was a center of art and Arabic learning; yet the empire soon crumbled because of its great size, social divisions, and religious conservatism. Externally, the Almohads were confronted by the Christian reconquest of Spain; their defeat at Las Navas de Tolosa in 1212 resulted in their total withdrawal from Spain. In North Africa, the empire divided into local kingdoms, called the Barbary States, one of which captured Marrakesh in 1269.

In the late 15th century, Christian Spain, having expelled the Muslims from the Iberian peninsula, captured several Algerian ports. The Christians were forced off the coast with Turkish assistance, and Algeria became nominally part of the Ottoman empire in 1518, although the local rulers had a high degree of autonomy. The Barbary States were in fact conquered for Turkey by a corsair, or pirate, known as Barbarossa, to prevent their falling to Christian Spain. Thereafter, the Barbary States became a base for piracy against European shipping in the

Opposite: **Stephen Decatur, who led the U.S. campaign against the Barbary pirates, meeting the** *dey* **of Algiers.**

Below: **Almohad expansion in North Africa.**

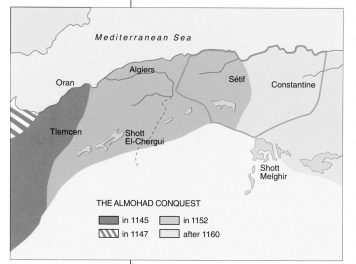

THE ALMOHAD CONQUEST

- in 1145
- in 1147
- in 1152
- after 1160

HILALIANS

Despite their immense influence, Arabs in the Maghrib represented only a small urban elite, whose detribalized members frequently married Berber women or took wives from their own narrow circle of Arab families, which were the products of generations of intermarriage with Berbers. From the 12th to the 14th centuries, however, Arabs of a distinctly different character, tribal people known collectively as the Hilalians, reached the Maghrib in large numbers, dramatically altering the face and culture of the region.

In the middle of the 11th century, the Fatimid caliph in Cairo invited the Bani Hilal and Bani Salim, Bedouin tribes originally from Hejaz and the Yemen who for years had ravaged upper Egypt, to migrate to the Maghrib and punish their rebellious vassals, the Zirids. The slow but continuous advance of these nomads across the region was, in the words of historian Ibn Kaldun, like a "swarm of locusts," impoverishing it, destroying towns, and turning farmland into steppes.

The Hilalian impact on the central Maghrib was devastating in both demographic and economic terms. Over a long period of time Arabs displaced Berber farmers from their land and converted it to pasturage. For the first time the extensive use of Arabic spread to the countryside. Sedentary Berbers who sought protection from the Hilalians were gradually Arabized. Others, driven from their traditional lands, joined them as nomads or fled to the mountains. Ironically, the first entry of these Arabs into Morocco in the 12th century coincided with a political and religious revival among the Berber tribal confederations.

Mediterranean. The booty and tribute paid to gain immunity from attacks was the chief revenue for local rulers.

Piracy against European shipping led to British and U.S. intervention in the early 19th century. In 1801, the United States, whose ships had been attacked, launched the Tripolitan War against Tripoli (now Libya). In 1815, the United States also fought against Algiers, which was bombarded by an Anglo-Dutch fleet in 1816. However, the piracy was only effectively ended with the French conquest of Algeria in 1830, and the deposition of the *dey* (regent) of Algiers.

Bomb damage during World War II. During the early years of the war, Algeria was under the Vichy administration. After 1942, it served as a major base for the Allied North Africa campaign. Algiers was the capital of free France until the liberation of Paris.

FRENCH RULE AND THE RISE OF NATIONALISM

France's campaign to conquer northern Algeria ended in 1847 with the defeat of Algerian leader Abd al-Qadir. In 1848 the area was declared part of France. Despite fierce resistance, the French pushed gradually southward until Algeria's current boundaries were drawn in 1902.

Organized Algerian nationalist movements arose after World War I under the leadership of two men: Messali Hadj, who desired complete independence; and the moderate Ferhat Abbas, who wanted France to live up to its assimilationist ideals. European settlers, however, resisted all efforts to grant political and economic equality to the Algerians.

World War II aroused nationalist hopes, and when these were not met, strife broke out in Algeria. In 1945, when Algerians demonstrated for independence in Sétif and Constantine, the police opened fire, killing thousands. In retaliation, Algerians organized armed groups and attacked colons. French reprisal was swift. Altogether 103 French and 8,000 Algerians were killed. Although the French government granted Algerians the right to vote on a separate electoral roll in 1947, demands for full political equality and further reform were opposed.

THE WAR OF INDEPENDENCE

French rule had produced an Algeria combining ultramodern and archaic aspects. European-style cities stood alongside centuries-old villages; large-scale agricultural units existed next to hundreds of tiny farms. More than a million European settlers *(colons)*—a majority of French origin—possessed the principal industrial, commercial, and agricultural enterprises. Most of the 8.5 million Muslims either pursued primitive economic activities or performed menial tasks in the modern sector. Despite reforms and despite the fact that Algeria was technically not a colony but comprised three departments of France, the Muslims were politically disadvantaged as well. They had equality before the law but little power to make or administer it.

Nationalist aspirations for liberation heightened Muslim discontent. A National Liberation Front (FLN, from its French name) was formed, and on November 1, 1954, small FLN bands began to raid French army installations and colons' holdings.

French colonists riot in Algiers in 1958 in reaction to France's inability to defeat the Algerian nationalists.

Ahmed Ben Bella was an idealist loved by the people of Algeria.

The FLN also used terroristic and revolutionary war tactics to force adherence by the Muslims or to dissuade them from apathy or sympathy toward the French. Terror begat terror; the French army responded with traditional and counter-revolutionary military methods. But the French had little success. Neither the military efforts of the 500,000 strong army nor sizable political concessions produced a decisive defeat of the rebels or the firm allegiance of the Muslim masses. By 1958 the Fourth Republic was at a stalemate—and crisis.

The colons and certain factions of the French army were alarmed by the ineffectiveness of the Paris government. On May 13, in Algiers, they rioted, overran the government offices, and established an emergency Committee of Public Safety. In Paris, Premier Pierre Pflimlin's ministry was paralyzed, and Charles de Gaulle was asked to become premier. He was granted emergency powers and the right to frame a constitution for a Fifth Republic.

In 1962, in the face of international disapproval and turmoil in France, de Gaulle finally announced a referendum on independence. After an overwhelming vote in favor of independence and in spite of violent protests by French nationals, Algeria became independent on July 5, 1962. Algeria was the last of the French holdings in North Africa to become independent, Tunisia and Morocco having achieved that status in 1956. After a power struggle within the FLN, Ahmed Ben Bella became Algeria's first president in 1963.

INDEPENDENCE AND AFTER

Confronting a society devastated by war and the subsequent flight of European capital and skilled workers, Ben Bella nationalized abandoned colonial holdings and announced his support of national liberation movements in other colonial lands. Conflict with Morocco, economic problems, and Ben Bella's dictatorial personality provoked a bloodless coup on June 19, 1965 led by Houari Boumedienne. Boumedienne maintained Algeria's image as an avant-garde Third World state and began its support of Polisario demands for an independent Western Sahara. His nationalization of French oil and natural gas concessions in 1971 symbolized Algeria's economic liberation, but Algeria still accepted French aid.

Chadli Bendjedid, who became president in 1979 after the death of Boumedienne and was elected in 1984 and 1988, maintained Algeria's prominence as a speaker for the Third World and pursued Maghrib unity. He liberalized the economy somewhat, but high unemployment, inflation, and corruption sparked massive unrest in October 1988.

In the June 1990 local elections—the first multiparty elections since 1962—the fundamentalist Islamic Salvation Front (FIS) won almost 65 percent of the vote. Violence by fundamentalists demanding an Islamic state led to the imposition of a state of siege from June to September 1991. After the FIS won the first round of delayed legislative elections in December, Bendjedid was forced to step down. The army seized control, cancelled the runoff elections, outlawed the FIS, and installed Mohammed Boudiaf as head of a new presidential council. Boudiaf was assassinated in June; it was unclear whether fundamentalists or FLN hardliners were responsible. Islamic fundamentalist extremists warned foreigners to leave Algeria or risk death. In January 1994, the military rulers named General Liamine Zéroual president, Algeria's fourth head of state in two years.

Houari Boumedienne led Algeria until his sudden death in 1979.

GOVERNMENT

THE NATIONAL LIBERATION FRONT (FLN, from its French name) led Algeria to independence and was the country's only legal political party until 1989. The 1963 constitution was suspended following a military coup in 1965. A 1976 constitution provided for a unicameral National Assembly and a powerful president. A new National Charter, approved in 1986, increased the role of the private sector and declared socialism and Islam to be the twin pillars of the state. In November 1988, after a wave of anti-government protests, voters overwhelmingly approved increasing the power of the prime minister, who was made responsible to the legislature, and reducing the role of the FLN. In February 1989, they approved a new constitution that paved the way for the July 1989 legalization of a multiparty system.

Opposite: **Soldiers on patrol. Terrorist violence has reached alarming proportions in recent years in Algeria.**

Left: **Women lined up to vote in the independence referendum.**

CIVIL WAR

Political, social, and economic problems have created a climate of violent unrest in Algeria. A state of emergency has been in effect since early 1992. Since September 1993, a terrorist campaign against foreigners has resulted in the deaths of over a hundred people. Assassinations of Algerian intellectuals, government officials, journalists, and military officers are frequent. Sporadic bombings, gun battles between government forces and insurgents, and other violence occur almost daily. Currently, Algerian military and other security personnel are unable to offer adequate protection.

The government of Algeria has imposed a rigorously enforced late-night curfew in the central region around Algiers. Roadblocks are located at many major intersections. Security personnel at roadblocks and intersections expect full cooperation with their instructions. In response, terrorist groups have set up false roadblocks as ambushes.

Over one hundred foreigners have been kidnapped and murdered since September 1993, sometimes in assaults involving dozens of attackers.

A terrorist attack at a pipeline facility south of Algiers resulted in the death of five expatriates. Terrorists have threatened to kill all foreigners who do not leave Algeria. An Air France flight was hijacked at Algiers Airport on December 24, 1994 by heavily armed terrorists who threatened to blow up the aircraft. Women have been a particular target of the terrorists, as have been intellectuals, writers, journalists, and artists.

By mid-1994, three special courts instituted to try suspects accused of terrorist offences had handed down some 490 death sentences, and a total of 26 executions had been carried out in an effort to curb the violence. Some sources estimate that the number of people killed since February 1992 may be as high as 50,000. Amnesty International has condemned the Algerian government for widespread use of torture and systematic killing of suspected militants.

Despite threats to their lives, 75 percent of Algerian citizens in Algeria and overseas disregarded the Islamists' calls to boycott the November 1995 elections and returned President Liamine Zéroual to power.

A march organized by the Islamic Salvation Front takes over the streets on April 20, 1990. This group was banned in 1992.

The Arabic text on the building reads: مؤتمر شهداء الثورة

Above: **The former building of the FLN party in Tizi-Ouzou in Kabylia.**

Opposite: **Former President Chadli Bendjedid. Under Bendjedid, constitutional referendums ended the commitment to socialism and the FLN's monopoly of power.**

GOVERNMENT STRUCTURE

The president is the head of state, head of the armed forces, and responsible for national defense. He must be Algerian, a Muslim, and at least 40 years old. His wife must also be Algerian. He is elected by secret ballot for a five-year term and can only be re-elected once. The president presides over a Council of Ministers and a High Security Council. He decides and conducts foreign policy. He appoints a prime minister, who initiates legislation and appoints a Council of Ministers. The prime minister is responsible to the National People's Assembly, whose 430 members are elected for a five-year term. When the Assembly is not in session, the president can legislate by decree, after consulting with the prime minister.

The National People's Assembly proposes and, with the Council of the Nation, ratifies laws. The Assembly has two ordinary sessions per year. The Assembly may be convened for an extraordinary session at the request of the president, the prime minister, or of two-thirds of its members. Both the prime minister and the Assembly may initiate legislation.

THE CONSTITUTION

The constitution can be revised on the initiative of the president by a two-thirds majority of the Assembly, and must be approved in a national referendum. The basic principles of the constitution may not be revised.

The state guarantees the inviolability of the home, of private life, and of the person. The state also guarantees the secrecy of correspondence, the freedom of conscience and opinion, freedom of intellectual, artistic, and scientific creation, and freedom of expression and assembly.

The state guarantees the right to form political associations, to join a trade union, the right to strike, to work, to protection, to security, to health, to leisure, and to education. It also guarantees the right to leave the national territory, within the limits set by law.

The constitution perpetuates the 1984 Family Code, which relegated Algerian women to the status of minors for life, restricts their rights, and maintains the legal supremacy of men over women. The constitution has named Islam as the state religion and Arabic as the only national language.

PRESIDENT LIAMINE ZÉROUAL

Head of state during half of Algeria's four-year conflict between Muslim fundamentalists and the authorities, Zéroual has been accused of being the "authorities' candidate." He claims he is an independent candidate for all Algerians. He tried twice to negotiate with detained Muslim fundamentalist leaders to end the violence. He blamed the failures on their "intransigence."

Zéroual joined the revolution against the French at age 16. In 1965, he went to the Soviet Union for military training and was then posted to head an artillery unit in western Algeria. In the 1980s, Zéroual commanded three of Algeria's military regions, becoming land forces chief in 1988. He resigned from the military in 1989 after a dispute with President Chadli Bendjedid and became ambassador to Romania before being named defense minister in July 1993.

POLITICAL PARTIES AND ELECTIONS

From independence until 1989, the National Liberation Front (FLN) was the only authorized political grouping, Algeria having been designated as a one-party state. Under constitutional changes approved in 1989, however, Algerians were permitted to form "associations of a political nature" as long as they did not "threaten the basic interests of the state" and were not "created exclusively on the basis of religion, language, region, sex, race, or profession." To operate legally, parties were also required to obtain government permits. The process of legalization began in August 1989, and multiparty activity was permitted for the first time at a local election in June 1990.

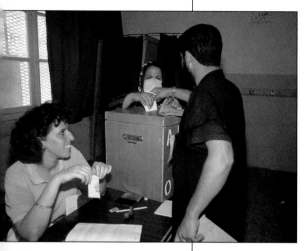

Voting in the 1990 election, the first in which multiple parties participated. By the end of June 1991, there were nearly 60 legal parties.

A new electoral law, adopted in 1990, introduced a system of partial proportional representation for local elections. This meant that any list of candidates obtaining more than 50 percent of the votes would win all the seats. If no party secured the requisite majority, the winning list would be allocated one-half of the seats, with the remainder proportionately distributed among other parties receiving at least seven percent of the vote.

SOME LEGAL PARTIES

NATIONAL LIBERATION FRONT (Front de Libération Nationale, FLN). For many years this was the only political party in Algeria. Now in decline, it nevertheless has members still entrenched in many formal and informal positions of local and national influence.

HAMAS PARTY (Mouvement pour la Société Islamique, MSL). An Islamic fundamentalist organization distinct from the more extreme Palestinian group of the same name. Hamas advocates "coexistence" with groups of opposing views and introducing "by stages" an Islamic state that would maintain "respect for individual liberties."

PARTY FOR THE ALGERIAN RENEWAL (PRI). Small, moderate fundamentalist group led by banker Noureddine Boukrouh. The government has promoted it as the legal alternative to the banned FIS.

SOCIALIST FORCES FRONT (FFS). Long clandestine, the predominantly Berber FFS was legalized in November 1989. It won 25 seats on a 15 percent vote share in the December 1991 first election round. Hocine Ait-Ahmed, who heads the FRS, was a leader of the 1954 Algerian revolution.

ILLEGAL GROUPS

ISLAMIC SALVATION FRONT (Front Islamique du Salut, FIS). The FIS was organized in 1989 to represent the surging Islamic fundamentalist movement. The party won 188 seats in the December 1991 first election round, and was preparing to launch the world's first Islamic state via the ballot box when the military took over. In March 1992, the Algerian courts formally banned the FIS upon petition of the High Council of State. It is generally believed that elements of the FIS were responsible for the emergence of armed splinter groups such as the GIA and the MIA.

Leader of the Islamic Salvation Front, Cheikh Abassi Madani, at a press conference in April 1990. It is unclear whether the FIS supports the GIA in its terrorist campaign.

ARMED ISLAMIC GROUP (GIA). The most militant of the underground fundamentalist organizations, the GIA has claimed responsibility for numerous kidnappings and killings and warned foreigners to leave Algeria. Its guerrilla force is estimated at 5,000–10,000 fighters.

ARMED ISLAMIC MOVEMENT (MIA). The MIA is the underground fundamentalist organization formed in response to the banning of the FIS in 1992. The MIA is described as less militant than the GIA.

ECONOMY

LESS THAN 20 PERCENT of Algeria's land, mostly along the coast, is arable. The country has petroleum deposits and the fourth largest natural gas reserves in the world. There are also deposits of iron ore, phosphates, mercury, and zinc.

During the colonial period, Algeria's major exports were wines and citrus fruits. The discovery of Saharan petroleum and natural gas in the mid-1950s accelerated French investment and initiated the ongoing transformation of the Algerian economy. Almost all foreign enterprises were nationalized after independence, including (in 1971) French oil and natural gas interests. The economy remains largely under state control, despite the return of some land and businesses to private hands in the 1980s. Algeria is dependent on oil and gas exports to finance internal development. The 1984–1989 Five-Year Plan encouraged private and foreign investment.

An estimated 28 percent of Algeria's workforce was unemployed in 1993.

Opposite: **A seamstress at work. Because state planning has generally been capital rather than labor intensive, there is severe under- and unemployment in some areas. Since 1980, however, more attention has been paid to agriculture, light industry, and the provision of human services.**

Left: **A small shop is open for business.**

Above: **An oil well in the Sahara.**

Opposite: **Tomatoes grown in a greenhouse.**

MINING AND INDUSTRY

Industry (including mining, manufacturing, construction, and power) contributed an estimated 46.6 percent of GDP in 1992, and engaged 31.2 percent of the employed population in 1987. The mining sector engaged only 1.6 percent of the employed population in 1987, but provided almost all of Algeria's export earnings. The major mineral exports are petroleum and natural gas. Reserves of iron ore, phosphates, lead, and zinc are also exploited. In addition, Algeria has deposits of antimony, tungsten, manganese, mercury, copper, and salt.

Manufacturing engaged 12.2 percent of the employed population in 1987 and provided an estimated 10.7 percent of GDP in 1992. The most important sectors are food processing, machinery, and transport equipment. There is a large steel works facility at Annaba, and trucks, textiles, cement, and paper are also major manufactures.

Energy is derived principally from natural gas and petroleum. These provide 98 percent of Algeria's export earnings, despite the decline of world energy prices in the 1980s. Algeria is a member of the Organization of Petroleum Exporting Countries (OPEC). Initial development plans concentrated on the development of heavy industry, particularly the building of ultramodern petrochemical and gas liquefaction complexes to complement Algeria's oil and natural gas fields. In 1986, Algeria produced 12.7 million kilowatt hours of electricity.

ORGANIZATION OF PETROLEUM EXPORTING COUNTRIES

The Organization of Petroleum Exporting Countries (OPEC) was created by Iran, Iraq, Kuwait, Saudi Arabia, and Venezuela in Baghdad on September 14, 1960, to counter oil price cuts of U.S. and European oil companies. Qatar joined in 1961, Indonesia and Libya in 1962, Abu Dhabi (now part of the United Arab Emirates) in 1967, Algeria in 1969, Nigeria in 1971, and Ecuador and Gabon in 1973. In 1979 OPEC countries produced 66 percent of world petroleum but by 1992 only 41 percent.

In its first decade OPEC limited itself to preventing reductions in the price of oil, but by 1970 it had begun to press for rate increases (there was a fourfold increase in 1973–1974 alone). Prices stabilized between 1974 and 1978 but increased by more than 100 percent during 1979. Demand slackened at the higher prices, and non-OPEC producers increased production. OPEC production quotas broke down during the 1980s, and there were disputes between nations seeking to curb production in hopes of driving prices up and those increasing production to avoid disrupting the world economy or to sustain earnings in the face of dropping prices. OPEC's influence continued to decline in the 1990s, and Ecuador withdrew from the organization on January 1, 1993.

AGRICULTURE

Agriculture (including forestry and fishing) is an important sector of the economy, employing 22.8 percent of Algeria's working population in 1993, and providing an estimated 15 percent of GDP. The principal crops are wheat, barley, and potatoes. Olives, citrus fruits, and grapes are also grown.

Despite the proclaimed 1971 "Agrarian Revolution," agricultural production increased only 0.2 percent between 1970 and 1979, and Algeria must still import 60 percent of its food. To boost food production and reduce unemployment, development plans since 1980 have invested heavily in agriculture, and many state controls have been relaxed.

Wine remains an important export, although the government has uprooted many vineyards because of Islamic prohibitions and replaced them with plantings of cereal crops. Other commercial crops are citrus fruits, vegetables, olives, figs, and dates. Livestock raising (mainly sheep and goats) provides a livelihood for nomads in sparsely settled semiarid areas.

There are several major ports in Algeria, which also has a fleet of tankers and a ferry service to France.

TRANSPORTATION AND TRADE

The French left an impressive infrastructure, which the Algerians have maintained and expanded. The excellent road system now includes a trans-Saharan highway connecting northern Algeria with the far south, and there are plans to increase the rail network. Major ports include Oran, Arzew, Bejaia, Skikda, and Annaba.

Although France remains the primary trading partner, Algeria has successfully diversified its markets. Other major trading partners are Italy, Germany, the United States, and the Netherlands. A trans-Mediterranean pipeline, completed in 1983, transports natural gas to Italy and other European markets; pipelines to Libya and Morocco are to be built. Petroleum and natural gas are exported to the United States and other nations. Algeria's principal exports are mineral fuels, lubricants (including petroleum and derivatives), vegetables, tobacco, hides, and dates. Principal imports include machinery and transport equipment, food, and basic manufactures.

THE 1990–1994 DEVELOPMENT PLAN

The government's principal aim in the 1990–1994 Development Plan was to liberalize the economy, allowing a greater measure of private enterprise and encouraging foreign investment. In an attempt to reduce its debt, Algeria was to pursue an aggressive policy in marketing hydrocarbons, especially natural gas, while promoting new hydrocarbon industries and agriculture. However, the prosperity of the Algerian economy continued to depend heavily on petroleum and natural gas prices.

The Algerian government hoped that credit arrangements made in the early 1990s with the International Monetary Fund, the World Bank, the European Community, and other bodies would reinforce the economy until petroleum prices made a recovery. By 1994, however, the government had failed to arrest Algeria's economic crisis, and the debt-ridden country faced the prospect of bankruptcy. In April 1994, the government came to an agreement with the IMF to implement a stabilization program in return for a standby credit of $1,040 million.

ALGERIANS

ALGERIANS ARE PRIMARILY of Arab, Berber, and mixed Arab-Berber descent. However, their mixed features reflect the considerable fusion of peoples that has gone into creating modern Algeria. Algerians range in coloring from the dark skin, negroid features, and kinky hair typical of many Tuareg, to the blond hair and Caucasian features of many Berbers. Since it is difficult to distinguish ethnic affiliation by physical features, language is the primary way Algerians tell communities apart. Berbers and Arabs have traditionally lived peacefully together, sharing their faith in Islam but following their different traditions.

The French population, approximately 10 percent of the total in colonial times, has since fallen to about one percent. Many other Europeans and almost all of the 150,000 Jews in Algeria also left the country after independence. More than one million Algerians live abroad, chiefly in France.

Opposite: **An old Berber woman with traditional tattoos decorating her face.**

Left: **Two Tuareg men converse in the desert. Tuareg men wear veils covering their faces, while the women expose their faces.**

ARABS

The term Arab refers to people who speak Arabic as their native language. A Semitic people, Arabs make up 70 percent of Algeria's population. The great majority of Arabs are Sunni Muslims.

References to Arabs as nomads and camel herders in northern Arabia appear in Assyrian inscriptions of the ninth century B.C. The name was subsequently applied to all inhabitants of the Arabian peninsula. From time to time Arab kingdoms arose on the fringes of the desert, but no great Arab empire emerged until Islam appeared in the seventh century A.D.

Almost half of all Arabs live in cities. Although traditional tribal life has nearly disappeared, tribal values and identity retain some importance, especially when linked to Islam. Descent from the clan of Prophet Mohammed or from one of the first Arab tribes to accept Islam still carries great prestige. Many villages and towns contain prominent families with common links to tribal ancestors. Blood ties contribute to the formation of political factions.

These types of relationships are less prevalent in cities; even there, however, leading families may seek to intermarry their children to preserve traditional bonds, and many urban families retain patronage ties to their villages.

MOORS

When the Arab armies swept across Northern Africa in the seventh century, they found indigenous tribespeople called Berbers living in the northwestern corner of the continent. After the Arabs converted many of the Berbers to Islam early in the eighth century, the Berbers and Arabs joined to conquer Spain. There they intermarried with the Spanish. Their descendants came to be called Moors. "Moor" generally refers to people of mixed ancestry who live along the seacoast of northwest Africa.

The Moors reached the height of their power in Spain. After the conquest of the Visigothic kingdom in 711 and a period of great disorder, the highly cultured Arab caliphate of Cordoba was formed (shown below is a school of Cordoba under the Moors). The caliphate lasted until 1031. Following its collapse, the Moors who controlled northwestern Africa crossed to Spain and took over.

After the battle of Las Navas de Tolosa in 1212, in which Alfonso VIII of Castile broke the Moorish power in central Spain, the Moors still ruled the kingdom of Granada. Granada rose to a splendor rivaling that of the former caliphate of Cordoba. Not until 1492 was this Moorish kingdom, weakened by internal discord, shattered by the armies of Ferdinand and Isabella. The Moors were then expelled from Spain.

The name Moor comes from the Latin Mauri, *the name for the Berber inhabitants of the old Roman province of Mauritania, the territory now covered by Morocco and part of Algeria.*

Opposite: **An Arab in a long robe that protects the clothes underneath from desert storms.**

Berbers generally have no sense of belonging to a Berber people or a nation, but have strong loyalties to village, clan, and tribe.

BERBERS

The name Berber refers to the descendants of the pre-Arab populations of North Africa. The Berbers are a composite people, presenting a broad range of physical features, and the bond among various Berber groups is almost entirely a linguistic one. The term comes from the derogatory Greek word for non-Greek and was taken into both Latin and Arabic, yielding the English term "barbarian."

Berbers are Caucasoid, frequently with blond hair, and speak variations of a single language, Berber. They call themselves by some variant of the word *amazigh*, which means "free man," and have no sense of community or ethnic unity beyond their tribal affiliations, which notably include the Kabyle of Algeria, the Riffians and Shluh of Morocco, and the Tuareg of the Sahara.

Berbers represent about 30 percent of Algeria's population, and mostly live in rural areas. Algeria's four main Berber groups—Kabyle, Shawiya, M'zabite, and Tuareg—are differentiated by dialect, cultural differences, and where they live.

Berber speakers, who today number about 25 million, are distributed through Libya, Tunisia, Algeria, Morocco, Mauritania, and the Western Sahara. Their density increases generally from east to west, but the Berber language is still retreating in favor of Arabic as the populations of the present nation-states become homogenized, although the Berbers have made many gains recently.

The maintenance of Berber language and identity carries with it social and cultural traits that conspicuously distinguish the Berbers from the surrounding Arabs. Despite great diversity, the Berbers generally are rural, either settled or nomadic, with an economy based on subsistence agriculture and animal husbandry. They are grouped territorially and governed in egalitarian districts run by councils, of which the head of each extended family is a member.

Berber tribes living in the mountain areas traditionally practice transhumance, moving up and down the mountains according to season to find the best pastures for their animals. While the bulk of the tribe moves with the herds, a small group stays behind to guard the collective granaries and grow some essential grains and vegetables.

Under French rule many Berbers, especially Kabyle, became part of the French-speaking elite who dominated Algerian politics and finance. The French, in a "divide and rule" policy, deliberately favored the Kabyles in education and employment. As a result, in the years after independence Kabyles moved into all levels of state administration across Algeria, where they remained a large and influential group.

Two Berber women. Berber women have a higher status generally than Arab women.

Girls playing in the Kabylian countryside.

"Follow the path of your father and grandfather" is an old Kabyle saying followed even today.

KABYLES The Kabyles, the largest Berber-speaking tribe in Africa, occupy the mountainous coastal area of Kabylia, in northern Algeria. They number approximately three million, and are most resistant to national government intrusion. Their historical origins, like those of other Berber peoples, are only vaguely known. Principally agriculturalists who cultivate cereal grains and olives, Kabyles also maintain their subsistence economy through goat herding. Villages of stone or chopped straw and clay are built on barren ridges or slopes overlooking gardens, orchards, and pastures. Many Kabyles have migrated to coastal cities or to France in search of employment, but they tend to stay together in clans.

Patrilineal clans characterize the marriage-family structure, with the husband's mother occupying a dominant position in the household. Councils composed of male elders govern each village, drawing upon a well-developed legal code to deal with property disputes and other offenses. Islam is the dominant religion, although Christianity is also found. Among rural populations, traditional beliefs in invisible beings and mysterious powers still persist. Their women are the most restricted of all Berbers. Since independence, their status has improved in terms of education and careers.

SHAWIYAS The Shawiyas have lived in the Aurès Mountains of eastern Algeria since the first wave of Arab invasions. Through the centuries, Shawiyas isolated their groups, either by farming in the north or following herds in the south. Only Kabyle peddlers or desert camel herders visited Shawiya villages. During the revolution, the French herded many anti-French Shawiyas into concentration camps, disturbing the seclusion that had lasted for centuries.

A group of Shawiya men. Shawiya men believe their women have special magical powers. This belief gives Shawiya women slightly more privileges than Kabyle women.

M'ZABITES Descendants of the Kharidjite refugees who fled the Fatimids, the M'zabites live behind seven walled cities along the northern Sahara near Wadi M'zab, which lent its name to the group. The M'zabites, like the Shawiyas, stay separate from the rest of the world. They call themselves "God's family." M'zabites follow a strict form of Islam and abide by their religious government of elders. M'zabite Islam provides social equality and literacy for men and women. However, women are not allowed to leave the oasis villages. Only M'zabite men can seek employment outside the village as merchants. By the mid-1980s, M'zabites built a retail trade that extended to Algiers. No matter where M'zabites live, however, they always return to the desert.

The Tuaregs have had to modify their lifestyle in the face of government restrictions.

TUAREGS The Tuaregs are the most independent of the Berber groups. Their name comes from *tarek*, meaning "those who abandoned God," and it was given by frustrated Muslim preachers who found these nomads unwilling to practice Islam centuries ago. Their free-wheeling desert culture, dominated by women, remained an oddity. Legend states that a Berber princess from Morocco journeyed across the severe desert with only her slave girl as companion. For her courage she was made leader—the first of a long line of women rulers. Tuareg women control the economy and property, and boys and girls study the Koran. Through the years, Tuareg men, but not women, wore veils. The custom proved practical as protection against sandstorms in the days when men roamed the Sahara on camels leading salt, gold, and date caravans.

Tuaregs traditionally range the Sahara through southern Algeria to northern Nigeria and from western Libya to Mali. Since the establishment of modern countries with firmly drawn borders, their traditional nomadic life has been severely restricted. The governments of Algeria and Niger, in particular, have limited the number of camel caravans allowed to pass the border each year. As a result, many Tuaregs moved south into Niger and Mali, but their numbers were depleted in the 1970s by disastrous droughts. Those who remained became semi-nomadic or even sedentary, tending their gardens around desert oases such as Tamanrasset. Today, some Tuaregs even work in Saharan gas and oil fields.

YVES SAINT LAURENT

Born in Oran on August 1, 1936, Yves Saint Laurent is a French fashion designer who furthered the trend for ready-to-wear clothes with his boutiques in Europe and the United States. The son of a successful French lawyer, he stayed in Algeria long enough to complete secondary school.

Saint Laurent left for Paris to pursue a career in designing women's clothes and costumes for the theater. After a *Vogue* magazine executive showed Christian Dior some of Saint Laurent's sketches in 1954, Dior hired him immediately as his assistant. On Dior's death in 1957, Saint Laurent was chosen head designer for the Dior establishment at the age of 21.

After induction into the French army and a nervous collapse, Saint Laurent opened his own Parisian fashion house in 1962 and in 1966 opened a series of boutiques that sold ready-to-wear designs. He also has marketed perfume and accessories. He is responsible for popularizing trousers for women for all occasions.

In 1983, the Metropolitan Museum in New York held a retrospective covering 25 years of Saint Laurent's work.

PIEDS-NOIRS

While Algeria was a department of France, many French families lived in Algeria. Those of French origin who were born in Algeria are called *pieds-noirs* ("pee-AY NWAH"), literally meaning "black feet," because the early French troops wore high black boots. Although many of them lived most of their lives in Algeria, they considered themselves to be French and identified with France.

At independence there were about one million expatriates in Algeria. As non-Muslims, this group had French citizenship. The non-Muslims felt more a part of European than Arab culture, and they fled Algeria in droves at independence. By the early 1980s there were only about 117,000 expatriates left in Algeria, of which 75,000 were European, including 45,000 French.

LIFESTYLE

ALGERIA INCLUDES within its borders many distinct lifestyles, ranging from members of the urban middle class, whose lifestyle differs from their counterparts in European countries principally in their religious practices, to nomads of the Sahara, whose lives follow a traditionally defined pattern quite foreign to most Westerners. Between these two extremes are the Berber villagers who constitute the bulk of Algerian society.

Fundamentally Berber in cultural and racial terms before the arrival of the Arabs and later the French, Algerian society was organized around extended family, clan, and tribe and was adapted to a rural rather than an urban setting. In the villages, family and Islamic tradition continue to determine the greatest part of people's lives. Agriculture remains the focus of economic activity.

In recent years, however, the lifestyles of Algerians have been disrupted by the civil war that has ravaged the country. Prominent public figures, intellectuals, journalists, as well as ordinary civilians have been the target of attacks by Islamic militants. Certain towns and entire neighborhoods in some cities have been virtually controlled by militants. Algerians who had followed a less strict form of Islam have been pressured to change their behavior under threat of death. Women and intellectuals have been the most directly affected by Islamicist pressure, but all feel its effects.

Above: **A Berber mother and daughters picking olives. For most people in the rural areas, family is the most important part of life.**

Opposite: **Women from three generations. Women's roles have undergone many changes since independence.**

Nomads in the Sahara follow a traditional lifestyle.

PREINDEPENDENCE ALGERIA

Before the French occupation in 1830, Algerians were divided between a few ancient cities and a sparsely settled countryside where subsistence farmers and nomadic herdsmen lived in small tribes. In the cities most people identified themselves by their ethnic or religious group rather than by class or economic standing. Social organization in the rural areas depended primarily on kinship ties. The basic kinship unit was the *ayla,* a small lineage the members of which claimed descent through the male line from a common grandfather or great-grandfather. Several ayla formed the larger lineage, the members of which traced their origin to a more remote male ancestor. Tribes were groups of clans claiming common or related ancestors or brought together by circumstance. The tribe had little political cohesion and tended to accept the authority of a chief only when faced with the danger of conquest or subjugation.

Settled Berber groups were democratic and egalitarian and were governed by a council composed of adult males. Social stratification of the kind found in Arab groups did not exist in Berber villages.

French rule and European settlement brought enormous social changes. Europeans took over the economic and political life of the country but remained socially aloof. Algerian urban merchants and artisans were squeezed out, and country landowners were dispossessed.

A rapid increase in population created tremendous pressure on agricultural lands. Villagers and tribespeople flocked to the towns and cities, where they formed an unskilled labor mass, scorned by Europeans and isolated from the clans that had given them security and a sense of solidarity.

This urban movement increased after World War I, and after World War II large numbers also migrated to France in search of work. The Kabyles were the principal migrants; during the 1950s as many as 10 percent of the people of Kabylia were working in France at any one time, and even larger numbers were working in cities of the Tell.

The European-Algerian dichotomy was the country's basic social division. The top echelon of the country included a few Algerians who had amassed land and wealth, a few respected Arabic scholars, and a few successful professionals. The small groups of prosperous Muslims never numbered more than about 50,000. Moreover, they lived in quarters of the cities separate from the Europeans and seldom intermarried.

Nomadic clans no longer holding sufficient flocks or territory had to accept the humiliation of settling in one place. This usually started with a few nomadic families settling on the outskirts of a town where they traded. Accepted eventually as part of the community by the original inhabitant clans, the former nomads often assumed as their own one of the traditional ancestors or saints of the community.

A modern urban apartment complex.

During the war of independence, women who were accustomed to a sheltered and segregated life found themselves suddenly thrust into revolutionary militancy.

THE REVOLUTION AND SOCIAL CHANGE

The war of independence resulted in dramatic social changes. Individuals developed new perceptions of themselves, their abilities, and their roles through wartime activities. Many young people struck out independently of their families, and new leaders emerged.

The eight-year war, stretching across most of the country, emptied many rural villages. In addition, almost three million Muslims were resettled by the French in "regroupment centers." Several of these became permanent settlements. As a result of these displacements, many lost their ties with the social groups the land had supported. French housing was suitable for the nuclear family rather than the traditional household, and those who had lived by subsistence farming became accustomed to functioning in a cash economy.

The destruction of the old communities particularly affected the lives of women, sometimes in contradictory ways. Released from the restraints imposed by family scrutiny, many women from rural villages, where wearing the veil was rare, adopted the veil voluntarily as a means of hiding themselves from the public eye.

Traditional relations between the generations were overturned, and class differences were submerged. The young could adapt to the new ways, but the old were ill-equipped for change and so relinquished much of their former prestige and authority. In addition, rural people for the first time came to know and desire such items as beds and shoes, and interest in comfort and consumption began to replace the frugality that had characterized traditional village life.

A MUDDLED TRANSITION

In the mid-1980s, Algerians were caught between a tradition that no longer commanded their total loyalty and a modernism that did not satisfy their needs. This dilemma especially affected the youth. Educated young women were pulled between the lure of study and a career and the demands of their husbands and fathers. Young men were torn between demands for fluency in modern Arabic and in French, and between devotion to Islam and the secularism of modernization. Above all loomed the reality of unemployment. Staggeringly high and with no real solution in sight, unemployment was a prime factor accounting for the boredom, frustration, and disillusionment that characterized the young generation.

Algerians also faced a cultural identity problem. Because colonialism had altered precolonial institutions and values, the country was faced with the task of building a national identity.

The government implemented a national program called the "cultural revolution" to mold an Algerian identity and personality. It aimed to recover and popularize the past, to Arabize the country through such measures as the substitution of Arabic for French, and in general to create a distinctive national personality with which the country as a whole could identify. This policy was not universally popular, particularly among the Kabyle Berbers, who sought to preserve their cultural and linguistic distinctiveness. Progress in the cultural revolution was modest at best because of the lack of funding and enthusiasm for it.

Algeria absorbed the heaviest impact of all Arab countries subject to European rule.

Above: **A Tuareg family. The traditional extended family consisted of grandparents, their married sons and families, unmarried sons, daughters if unmarried or divorced or widowed, with their children, and occasionally other related adults.**

Opposite: **Algerians have been guaranteed free medical care since 1974, although the medical system is still handicapped by a lack of doctors and facilities. Particular emphasis is placed on preventive medicine.**

FAMILY AND HOUSEHOLD

Before independence the basic Algerian family unit, particularly in the countryside, was the extended family. The senior male member exercised undisputed authority. Each married couple usually had their own room opening onto the family courtyard and prepared their own meals. Children were raised by all members of the group, who passed on to them the concept and value of group solidarity.

In recent years, particularly since independence, there has been a trend toward nuclear family units. The tendency has been for separate units to form at the marriage of a young man who could afford to set up a household for himself and his bride or on the death of the head of an extended family. In addition, there has been a developing tendency for wives to leave the household to perform labor seasonally or for a longer period. In the mid-1980s smaller families were especially favored by the young and the better educated.

HEALTH

In 1974, a new system of virtually free national health care was introduced. Hospitalization, medicines, and outpatient care were free to all, the cost borne equally by the state and social security. In 1984, the government adopted a plan to transform the health sector from a curative system to a preventive one more suitable to the needs of a young population. Rather than investing in expensive hospitals, health centers and clinics were to be emphasized along with vaccination programs. It was hoped that the infant mortality rate could be cut in half.

Tuberculosis, trachoma, venereal infections, and typhoid were the most serious diseases; gastrointestinal complaints, pneumonia, diphtheria, scarlet fever, and mumps were relatively common. Tuberculosis was considered the most serious health hazard, and trachoma ranked next; only a small minority of the population were entirely free from this fly-borne eye infection, which was directly or indirectly responsible for most of the numerous cases of blindness. Malaria and poliomyelitis, both formerly endemic, had been brought under control.

FAMILY PLANNING

The average Algerian woman has between seven and nine children. With 3.2 percent growth each year, Algeria is one of the faster growing nations. In the 20 years following independence, Algeria doubled its population. If the current growth rate continues, there is concern that the country's economic growth will be endangered. Already food, housing, and jobs are limited.

Although Algeria was slow to introduce family planning, the need eventually became evident. By the mid-1980s, programs had begun to meet with some success. The demand for information about family planning reportedly outstripped supply in some areas. It was estimated that about 10 percent of the population between the ages of 15 and 49 was using some form of contraception, and the government was increasing its publicity to encourage still greater participation.

MEN AND WOMEN

Roles for men and women are well defined in Algerian society. The honor of the family depends largely on the conduct of its women, particularly of sisters and daughters; consequently, women are expected to be decorous, modest, and circumspect. The slightest implication of unavenged impropriety, especially if publicly acknowledged, can irreparably damage the family's honor. If they discover a transgression, men are traditionally bound to punish the offending woman.

Upon marriage the bride often goes to the household, village, or neighborhood of the bridegroom's family, where she may be a stranger and where she lives under the critical surveillance of her mother-in-law. A great deal of marital friction centers on the difficult relationship between mother-in-law and daughter-in-law.

Because a woman begins to gain status in her husband's home when she produces sons, mothers love and favor their boys, often nursing them longer than girls. The relation between mother and son is warm and intimate, while the father is more distant.

About 50 percent of women in larger cities wear veils outside the home. There was a growing trend since independence of unveiling. However, it reversed slightly as more incidents of attacks on unveiled women by Islamic extremists made news. In remote rural areas veils are less important but outsiders rarely see women at all.

The greatest battle for women's rights was fought over the family code. For years the government tried to advance the legal status of women, but Muslim fundamentalists saw any changes as moves to Westernize Algerian family life. Bendjedid put aside the first draft of the code in 1982 because of opposition from vocal women's groups, yet two years later a more conservative version was passed without debate. Although women gained rights to child custody and to their dowries, the code guaranteed men's authority over divorce and whether women work outside the home.

Equality is far in the future for most Algerian women. Still, women have made some progress. Women can vote and run for office and the number of female wage earners has increased considerably since independence. Some moderate Islamist leaders have publicly defended the right of women to work. About seven percent of the workforce are women. Many of them are trained and employed in the fields of medicine, education, and the media; some women serve in the armed forces. As of 1985, only one woman had attained the rank of government minister.

ACTIVISTS AND WOMEN'S RIGHTS UNDER ATTACK

Nabila Djahnine, aged 35, an architect who led an organization called Tighri n Tmettut (Cry of Women, in Berber), was gunned down on February 15, 1995 by two men in a car as she walked to work. The murder is believed to have been committed by Islamist militants.

Since the cancellation of parliamentary elections in 1992, there has been fighting between the Algerian government and the armed Islamist opposition. Increasingly, women have been the targets of such violence. Women who work outside the home have been threatened and killed by Islamist militants. Women have been threatened with violence if they refuse, or, in other cases, if they choose, to wear the veil. Other women have been threatened with death because of their own or family members' identification with the government or security forces. Algerian defenders of women's rights believe that the armed Islamist groups target women as important cultural symbols: by driving women from the streets, the Islamist militants demonstrate their power to impose the culture they envision for Algeria.

Djahnine, a well-known activist in Tizi-Ouzou since she was a student, helped start a magazine called *Voice of Women* in 1990. In her writing, she defended Algerian women's right to participate in the civil and political life of their country. Despite escalating attacks on activists known for their opposition to the agenda of the armed Islamist militants, Djahnine remained an outspoken advocate for women's rights. Djahnine's organization has called for the elimination of discriminatory provisions from Algeria's family code.

MARRIAGE

Marriage was traditionally a family rather than a personal affair and was intended to strengthen already existing families rather than to establish new ones. The mass media popularized the notion of romantic love, but this has had little influence on marriage arrangements. Because the sexes do not ordinarily mix socially, young men and women have few or no acquaintances among the opposite sex. Parents arrange marriages for their children, finding a mate either through their own contacts or through a professional matchmaker.

Opposite: **A couple in traditional Berber dress. Berber women do not wear the veil.**

An Islamic marriage is a civil contract rather than a sacrament. The representatives of the bride's interests negotiate a marriage agreement with representatives of the bridegroom. Although the future spouses must, by law, consent to the match, they usually take no part in the arrangements. The contract establishes the terms of the union and outlines appropriate recourse if they are broken.

DRESS

Algerian clothing is a blend of Western style and Islamic custom, especially in cities.

Traditional dress for women and girls involves draping a long piece of cloth over the entire body into a *haik*. Haiks go over the head to hide the lower part of the face and cover the clothes underneath. Many rural women also hang charms around their neck to ward off the "evil eye" that brings bad luck. Traditional Berber dress varies from region to region, but generally consists of long skirts, blouses, and shawls with floral patterns, stripes, or embroidery in bright colors. In cities, younger women wear Western dress. As a compromise, some religious yet modern women wear a black or white veil covering their lower face.

Most men and boys in cities wear variations of Western-style clothing. They have shirts, jackets, and either Western-style or fuller pants. Businessmen wear suits and maybe a fez, the felt hat worn by North African Muslim men. In villages, men can be seen in a long hooded robe called a *burnous* ("BUHR-noos"), made of linen for summer and wool for winter. Tuareg men wrap five yards of indigo blue material around the head into a turban that also goes over their robes, hiding all but their eyes.

HOUSING

The Algerian housing problem has been less pressing than in many other developing countries owing to the post-independence flight of most of the Europeans. Nearly all the Europeans had been city dwellers, living in the new towns surrounding the medinas (traditional cities) that housed the Algerian population. Many simply abandoned their properties to squatters from the countryside. Sometimes as many as six Algerian families lived in a residence that formerly housed a single European family.

The most conspicuous development in rural housing during the post-independence years has been the One Thousand Socialist Villages project undertaken in 1972. According to the plan, each village would have a population of as many as 1,500 people in 200 houses, along with schools and clinics. Each unit had three rooms and was provided with electricity, heat, and running water. By mid-1979 about 120 villages had been completed. However, villagers were not invariably enthusiastic, and the village project has done little to slow migration to urban areas.

Nomads and Kabyllan mountain villagers have houses different from the Algerian norm. Nomads of the High Plateau and Sahara weave goats' hair, wool, and grass into dark-colored tents. In Kabylia, one-room homes on a mountaintop are built of clay and grass or piled stones. A low wall splits the room into one section for the family and another for animals.

In the mid-1980s urban housing varied from the most modern apartment buildings and private dwellings of concrete and glass to crowded shantytowns. The cities had grown so rapidly that the small-windowed walls and courtyards of the medinas occupied only a small fraction of the urban area. The most common rural dwellings were called *gourbi* ("GOHR-be"), some of which were huts constructed of mud and branches. Others were more solidly built with walls of stone or clay, and contained several rooms. Tiled or tin roofs were usually flat; but in parts of eastern Algeria subject to heavy rainfall or winter snows, the roofs were steeply slanted.

With the heavy urban migration of the early post-independence years, entire gourbi settlements appeared in Annaba and other coastal cities. During this period Kabylia was the only part of Algeria to enjoy a housing boom. A large majority of the emigrant laborers in France were Berbers from Kabylia, and the funds remitted by them to their families at home made the surge of building possible in this otherwise impoverished region.

Algerians value their privacy, so they surround their homes and gardens with high walls. A heavy door in a wall opens to a corridor that leads to a bright patio with a flower bed or fountain.

INSIDE AN ALGERIAN HOUSE

Everyday living rooms of the house encircle the patio. A receiving room for guests doubles as a dining room. Usually walls are whitewashed. The upper part of the walls and ceilings in older homes are covered with ornate mosaics and tiles. Lower walls are kept plain except for occasional family pictures. Family bedrooms and a kitchen complete the circle. If the family is wealthy, there may be a second patio with separate quarters for women and children.

High-rise buildings, Socialist villages, farmhouses, and tar paper shantytowns on urban fringes all have the same general plan of rooms surrounding a central open area. Even in mud and brick oasis homes, women work within a sheltered courtyard.

EDUCATION

Segregated schooling of French and Algerian children was abolished in 1949, and increases in Muslim enrollments were scheduled in the comprehensive 1954 Constantine Plan for betterment of Muslim living conditions. On the eve of independence, however, the European-oriented curriculum was still taught exclusively in French, and less than one-third of the school-age Muslim children were enrolled in schools at the primary level. At the secondary and university levels, only 30 percent and 10 percent of the students, respectively, were Algerians.

Algerian authorities set out to redesign the system to make it more appropriate to the needs of a developing nation. The hallmarks of their program were democratization, Arabization, and an emphasis on scientific and technical studies. Translated into practice, they sought an increase in literacy, free education, compulsory primary enrollment, replacement of foreign teachers and curricula, and the use of Arabic in place of French.

In the mid-1970s the primary and middle educational

Two boys on their way to school in Kabylia.

levels were reorganized into a nine-year system of compulsory basic education. Thereafter, at the secondary level, pupils followed one of three tracks—general, technical, or vocational—and then sat for the baccalaureate examination before going on to one of the universities, state technical institutes, or vocational training centers, or directly to employment. Attendance approached 90 percent in urban centers and 67 percent in rural areas. Teachers were nearly all Algerian, and instruction was entirely in Arabic, French being introduced only in the third year.

French continued as a primary language of instruction in secondary schools, particularly in mathematics and science. However, enrollments still fell short of planned targets, especially in scientific and technical fields.

LITERACY

Literacy programs for adults were initiated after 1962, when the national literacy rate was below 10 percent. The Conquest of Literacy program was mounted to help people attain literacy in either Arabic or French. Volunteer teachers held classes on the job, in homes, and in abandoned

A sign explains appropriate attire in a language clear to all. Illiteracy remains high in Algeria.

buildings; old French or Arabic grammar books, copies of the Koran, and political tracts were pressed into service as texts. Wide-ranging approaches, including correspondence courses and use of the public media, were introduced during the Second Four-Year Plan (1974–1977). Major responsibility for out-of-school education was assigned to two specialized government agencies given technical assistance under the second of three educational loans, but the main emphasis of the government's educational program has been on the rapid development of the formal school system.

Nevertheless, progress in literacy has been noteworthy. Forty-two percent of the population was literate in 1977. By 1991, the rate of adult illiteracy had declined to 42.3 percent (30.2 percent for men and 54.5 percent for women), still an uncomfortably high rate. The problem of combating illiteracy among adults has been sharpened by the fact that the need to achieve complete adult literacy is clearly secondary to education of the young.

RELIGION

ALMOST ALL ALGERIANS are Muslim. While the constitution declares Islam to be the state religion, it prohibits discrimination based on religious belief. The government protects the rights of the small Christian and Jewish populations and often includes leaders of these communities at ceremonial state functions.

The Jewish community numbers approximately 1,000 and maintains a synagogue in central Algiers. Since the departure of the French, Christianity is a peripheral religion. Algerian Christians reportedly number fewer than 1,000 and often worship only in private. Both Roman Catholic and Protestant churches are found in Algiers, primarily serving the foreign Christian community. Conversion from Islam to Christianity is extremely rare and is severely sanctioned by the Muslim community. Algerians who convert from Islam do so clandestinely.

The relationship between religion and state has always been close in Algeria. The Islamic clergy receives religious training administered by the government, and the Ministry of Religious Affairs appoints imams (Muslim religious leaders) to both state and privately funded mosques. On at least three occasions in 1993, pro-government imams were assassinated. Also during the year, several imams were reportedly removed from their positions for preaching antigovernment views, and Friday sermons at larger mosques were reportedly monitored by security forces, leading regime critics to argue that their freedom of religion had been compromised.

Above: **The mosque minaret in Tlemcen.**

Opposite: **A man recites from the Koran.**

75

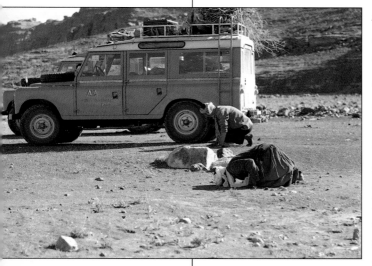

The believer must pray in a prescribed manner after purification through ritual ablutions at dawn, midday, midafternoon, sunset, and nightfall.

BASIC TENETS OF ISLAM

The *shahadah* (testimony) states the central belief of Islam: "There is no god but God (Allah), and Mohammed is his Prophet." This simple profession of faith is repeated on many ritual occasions, and recital in full sincerity identifies one as a Muslim. "Islam" means submission to God, and one who submits is a Muslim. Mohammed is the "seal of the Prophets;" his revelation completes the series of Biblical revelations received by the Jews and the Christians. God is believed to have remained the same throughout time, but people had strayed from his true teachings until set right by Mohammed.

Islam stands on five pillars: To witness that there is no God but Allah and that Mohammed is his Prophet, to perform the required prayers, to pay the *zakat* (charity dues), to fast during the month of Ramadan, and to perform the pilgrimage to Mecca (*hajj*). Whenever possible, men pray in congregation at the mosque under an imam, or prayer leader, and on Friday they are obliged to do so. Women may also attend public worship at the mosque, where they are segregated from the men, although most frequently they pray in seclusion at home.

In the early days of Islam the authorities imposed a tax on personal property proportionate to one's wealth; this was distributed to the mosques and to the needy. However, while still a duty of the believer, almsgiving has become a more private matter.

The ninth month of the Muslim calendar is Ramadan, a period of obligatory fasting in commemoration of Mohammed's receipt of God's revelation, the Koran. During this month, all but the sick and certain others are enjoined from eating, drinking, or smoking during daylight hours.

Finally, all Muslims at least once in their lifetime should, if possible, make the *hajj* to the holy city of Mecca to participate in special rites held at several spots there during the 12th month of the lunar calendar.

OBSERVANCE OF ISLAM

Although most Algerians are Sunni Muslims, there is much diversity in individual beliefs and practices. On the whole, people are conscious of the five pillars of Islam, whether or not they adhere to them, and consider many of their social norms and values part of their religion. The giving of alms, no longer enforced through taxation, is practiced to a lesser degree than before. Generosity toward the needy, however, remains one of the most important Algerian virtues. Dietary prohibitions are less generally observed in cities, and consumption of alcoholic beverages is sufficient to cause concern.

The mosque in Algiers. The *muaddhin* recites the call to prayer from the tower at the appropriate hours; those out of ear-shot determine the proper time by the sun.

The adherents of Islam, however, feel pride in their faith, assured they are the chosen people of God. They repeat the confession of faith regularly—at times of prayer, at ceremonies, and at other times in their lives. Such phrases as "it is God's will," "in the name of God," and "you, my servant, work, and I, God, will help you" are heard frequently. Although secular attitudes have spread at the expense of traditional Muslim ritual and social law, a nonpracticing Muslim is not necessarily to be considered an atheist or nonreligious.

A Muslim's first duty is to his or her immediate family. Islam induces feelings of moral responsibility and fosters the capacity for self-control.

Islam tries to generate kindness, generosity, mercy, sympathy, peace, disinterested goodwill, scrupulous fairness, and truthfulness towards all creation in all situations.

SOCIAL RESPONSIBILITIES OF MUSLIMS

The teachings of Islam concerning social responsibilities are based on kindness and consideration of others. Since an injunction to be kind is likely to be ignored in specific situations, Islam lays emphasis on specific acts of kindness and defines the responsibilities and rights of various relationships. In a widening circle of relationship, Muslims' first obligation is to their immediate family, then to other relatives, neighbors, friends and acquaintances, orphans and widows, the needy of the community, fellow Muslims, all humans, and animals.

Respect and care for parents is an important part of a Muslim's expression of faith. The Koran says: "Your Sustainer has decreed that you worship none but Him, and that you be kind to parents. Whether one or both of them attain old age in your lifetime, do not say to them a word of contempt nor repel them, but address them in terms of honor. And, out of kindness, lower to them the wing of humility and say: My Sustainer! Bestow on them Your mercy, even as they cherished me in childhood." (17:23-24) Regarding the duty toward neighbors: "He is not a believer who eats his fill when his neighbor beside him is hungry; and He does not believe whose neighbors are not safe from his injurious conduct."

Muslims have a moral responsibility not only to their parents, relatives, and neighbors but to all humans, animals, and useful trees and plants. For example, hunting of birds and animals for the sake of game is not permitted. Similarly, cutting trees and plants that yield fruit is forbidden unless there is a very pressing need for it.

HUMAN RIGHTS IN AN ISLAMIC STATE

THE SECURITY OF LIFE AND PROPERTY In the Prophet's address during his final pilgrimage, he said, "Your lives and properties are forbidden to one another till you meet your Lord on the Day of Resurrection." He also said, "One who kills a man under covenant (i.e., a non-Muslim citizen of a Muslim land) will not even smell the fragrance of Paradise."

THE PROTECTION OF HONOR The Koran does not allow one's personal honor to be abused: "O You who believe, do not let one set of people make fun of another set. Do not defame one another. Do not insult by using nicknames. Do not backbite or speak ill of one another." (49:11)

SANCTITY AND SECURITY OF PRIVATE LIFE The Koran guarantees privacy: "Do not spy on one another and do not enter any houses unless you are sure of their occupant's consent."

SECURITY AND PERSONAL FREEDOM Islam prohibits the imprisonment of any individual before his guilt has been proven before a public court. This means that the accused has the right to defend himself and to expect fair and impartial treatment from the court.

FREEDOM OF EXPRESSION Islam allows freedom of thought and expression, provided that it does not involve spreading that which is harmful to individuals and the society at large. For example, the use of abusive or offensive language in the name of criticism is not allowed. In the days of the Prophet, Muslims used to ask him about certain matters. If he had received no revelation on that particular issue, they were free to express their personal opinions.

FREEDOM OF ASSOCIATION The formation of associations, parties, and organizations is allowed, on the understanding that they abide by certain general rules.

FREEDOM OF CONSCIENCE AND CONVICTION The Koran states: "There should be no coercion in the matter of faith." Totalitarian societies of all ages have tried to deprive individuals of their freedom by subordinating them to state authority. Islam forbids such practice. Along with the freedom of conviction and freedom of conscience, Islam guarantees to the individual that his religious sentiments will be given due respect and nothing will be said or done that may encroach upon his right.

THE RIGHT TO BASIC NECESSITIES OF LIFE Islam recognizes the right of the needy to demand help from those who are more fortunate: "And in their wealth there is acknowledged right for the needy and the destitute."

In recent years, fundamentalist Muslims have forced women to veil themselves.

ISLAM AND THE ALGERIAN STATE

Algeria's relationship with Islam has been complex and turbulent. The socialist government vigorously suppressed any Islamic activism throughout the 1960s and 1970s. Many government workers and other employees judiciously kept clean-shaven to avoid overt identification with Islamicists.

However, under Boumedienne the government asserted state control over religious activities. This policy did not, however, mean any change in the standing of Islam as the state religion. Boumedienne insisted upon rigid observance of the holy month of Ramadan and its fast. Similarly, he discouraged production and consumption of wine and decreed a change in the weekend from Saturday/Sunday to Thursday/Friday, much to the dismay of government technocrats and the commercial classes. Although the Boumedienne regime consistently sought, to a far greater extent than its predecessor, to increase Islamic awareness and reduce Western influence, the rights of non-Muslims continued to be respected.

During the 1970s, what may be termed an Islamic "revival" began, an outgrowth of popular disenchantment with industrialization, urbanization, and the problems of a developing society. Manifestations of the revived interest in Islam could be detected in increased mosque attendance; in requests for prayer rooms in factories, offices, and universities; and in a spectacular increase in pilgrimages to Mecca. The movement was especially strong among the young, enjoyed the support of Islamic fundamentalists, and was responsible for a modification of the government's religious policies.

A mass public prayer in Algeria. Religion has become a powerful force in contemporary Algeria.

In the mid-1980s, the Ministry of Religious Affairs continued to dominate the religious sphere, controlling an estimated 5,000 public mosques and supervising religious education. The ministry provided guidance on sermons and sought to keep dissent out of mosques. The 5,000 practicing imams were paid by the state even as religious authorities admitted that 60 percent of them possessed inadequate training or were actually illiterate. At the same time, the government took steps to curb corruption in its ranks and committed itself to construct 160 new mosques and a large number of religious schools as part of its 1980–1984 development plan. Its decision to slow industrialization, although not religious in inspiration, appealed to those who wished to reduce the inflow of Western technology and cultural norms.

MARABOUTS

Persons who were remarkable in one way or another and consequently were believed to have *baraka* (special blessedness or grace) were called marabouts. This special status could be acquired by temporal leaders who commanded the respect of their followers, performed acts of charity, and had a reputation for justness, or by spiritual leaders who had studied in Koranic schools, had admirable personal qualities, and could perform miracles. Marabout status could also be acquired by having baraka bestowed by a marabout or by dying heroically. Marabouts were North African holy men, frequently described by English-language writers as saints. They had no place in pristine Islam and were looked on with disfavor by the orthodox.

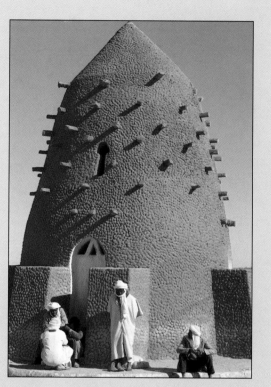

Brotherhoods of disciples frequently formed around particular marabouts, especially those who preached an original *tariqa,* a mystical or devotional "way." Each founder, an obvious possessor of great baraka, ruled an order of adepts who were ordinarily organized hierarchically. Before the 20th century, marabouts and their followers played significant political and moral roles, especially in western Algeria.

In the mid-1980s several of the maraboutic brotherhoods were still alive, although their membership had declined and some had been abolished by government decree. Nonetheless, veneration of marabouts and other glorified leaders was common throughout the Maghrib, and some observers saw maraboutic leaders as having regained some influence in rural areas since independence. Shrines had been established at the place of death of a leader or marabout or at some place associated with an event in his life, and every village and city or portion of a city had its patron saint or saints, who epitomized Muslim virtues and whose saintliness had been transformed into magical baraka at his special shrine (a shrine at Timimoun is shown above). The influence of marabouts and brotherhoods has now declined, and none of the postindependence regimes has had any interest in their revival because they represent fragmentation and disunity.

Many Algerians also accept the presence of mysterious powers and invisible beings. These might be benevolent or malevolent and must, as appropriate, be greeted, honored, propitiated, or avoided. Particularly in the countryside, Islam was mixed with a variety of pre-Islamic beliefs and practices. These included magic, various agricultural rites, and fear of the evil eye.

THE PEOPLE OF THE BOOK

The Prophet enjoined his followers to convert the infidel to the true faith. He specifically exempted, however, the "People of the Book"—Jews and Christians—whose religions he recognized as the historical basis of Islam. These peoples were to be permitted to continue their own communal and religious life, as long as they recognized the temporal domain of Muslim authorities, paid their taxes, and did not proselytize or otherwise interfere with the practice of Islam.

Soon after arriving in Algeria, the Christian colonists set about taking over the society. Although the Koran specifically discusses the position and treatment of subject Christians and Jews in a Muslim society, it makes no mention of the reverse possibility. A Muslim society permanently subject to non-Muslims is by its nature an affront to Islam and a reproach to Muslims who permit it to persist; it must be ended as quickly as possible and the supremacy of Islam restored. For this reason, among others, the religious movement was a factor in Algerian nationalism.

At independence, there were large Jewish and Christian communities. The Jewish community in Algeria is of considerable antiquity. Some members claim descent from Palestinian immigrants in pre-Roman times and a majority from refugees from Spanish persecution early in the 15th century. They had numbered well in excess of 100,000 before the Algerian revolution, but at independence in 1962 nearly all of them departed. Because the Cremieux Decrees of 1870 had granted them full French citizenship, most of the Jews went to France.

The government of independent Algeria discouraged anti-Semitism, and the small remaining Jewish population appears to have stabilized at roughly 1,000. The only remaining synagogue in Algiers was sacked by a group of youths in early 1977.

Around A.D. 100, Romans banished Jews from Europe to North Africa. Many Berbers converted to Judaism.

A small Christian shrine. Christianity came to Algeria very early in its history.

CHRISTIANITY

Christianity came to North Africa in the Roman era. Its influence declined during the chaotic period of the Vandal invasions but was strengthened in the succeeding Byzantine period, only to be eliminated after the Arab invasions of the seventh century.

The Roman Catholic Church was introduced after the French conquest of Algeria. The diocese of Algiers was established in 1838. Proselytization of the Muslim population was at first strictly prohibited, and few conversions were accomplished at any time. The several Roman Catholic missions established in Algeria were concerned with charitable and relief work; the establishment of schools, workshops, and infirmaries; and the training of staff for the new establishments. Some of the missionaries of these organizations remained in the country after independence, working among the poorer segments of the population. There is also a small Protestant community.

SAINT AUGUSTINE OF HIPPO

Saint Augustine (354–430) was one of the foremost philosopher-theologians of early Christianity and, while serving as bishop of Hippo Regius (modern Annaba, Algeria), the leading figure in the church of North Africa. He had a profound influence on the subsequent development of Western thought and culture and, more than any other person, shaped the themes and defined the problems that have characterized the Western tradition of Christian theology. Among his many writings considered classics, the two most celebrated are his semiautobiographical *Confessions*, and *City of God*, a Christian vision of history.

Augustine was born at Thagaste (modern Souk-Ahras, Algeria), a small town in the Roman province of Numidia. The first part of Augustine's life can be seen as a series of attempts to reconcile his Christian faith with his Roman culture. His mother, Saint Monica, a Christian Berber, had raised him as a Christian.

He received a classical education that schooled him in Latin literature. As a student in Carthage, he encountered the classical ideal of philosophy's search for truth and was fired with enthusiasm for the philosophic life. Unable to give up Christianity altogether, however, he adopted Manichaeism, a Christian heresy claiming to provide a rational Christianity on the basis of a purified text of Scripture. Trained at Carthage in rhetoric (public oratory), he became a teacher of rhetoric in Carthage, Rome, and finally Milan.

In Milan he discovered, through a chance reading of some books of Neoplatonism, a form of philosophy that seemed compatible with Christian belief. At the same time, he found that he was at last able to give up the ambitions for public success that had previously prevented him from embracing the philosophic life. In 386, Augustine underwent religious conversion. He retired from his public position and received baptism from Ambrose, the bishop of Milan. With a small group of friends, he returned to North Africa and, in Thagaste, established a religious community dedicated to the intellectual quest for God.

Augustine's ordination, unexpectedly forced upon him by popular acclamation during a visit to Hippo in 391, brought about a fundamental change in his life and thought. He eventually succeeded in bringing together the philosophic Christianity of his youth and the popular Christianity of his congregation in Hippo.

His subsequent career as priest and bishop was to be dominated by controversy and debate. Especially important were his struggles with the Donatists and with Pelagianism. In both of these controversies, Augustine opposed forces that set some Christians apart from others on grounds either of religious exclusivism or of moral worth.

LANGUAGE

LANGUAGE IS THE PRIMARY WAY Algerians tell ethnic communities apart. Before the Arab invasions, all groups spoke some form of Berber. Arabic encroached gradually, spreading through the areas most accessible to migrants and conquerors. Berber remained the mother tongue in many rural areas. Later, when France took control of Algeria, French was made the first language. Algerians continued to speak Arabic and Berber in their homes as a form of protest.

Today, Arabic is the official national language and the language of the majority of Algerians. Speaking and writing Arabic identifies Algerians with Islam, Arab culture, and other Arab countries. A modern form of Arabic is used for radio, television, theater, and public speaking.

Reorienting society to Arabic has been a slow process. The four main Berber groups continue to use their own dialects, and French persists as a necessity for some businesses and in technical and scientific fields. Of the three radio networks, each broadcasts in a different language—Arabic, French, and Tamazight (the Berber language). French is being phased out, although it is still taught as a second language in schools because of its usefulness in an international setting.

Language has been a focal point of ethnic conflict in Algeria in recent years. Berber resistance to "Arabization" has focused on demands for recognition of Tamazight as an official language alongside Arabic.

Above: **A street sign is located in an unlikely spot—the middle of the desert.**

Opposite: **Two women converse in the marketplace. Dialectical Arabic and Berber dialects are the main languages spoken in Algeria.**

بنـــك الفلاحـة والتنميـة الريفيــة

BANQUE DE L'AGRICULTUE ET DU DEVELOPPEMENT RURAL

The modern variety of written Arabic, which can be called literary Arabic, is grammatically simpler than classical Arabic and is sometimes written with vowels.

ARABIC AND BERBER

Arabic is a Semitic tongue related to Hebrew, Aramaic, and Amharic. The dominant language throughout North Africa and the Middle East, Arabic was introduced to the coastal regions by the Arab conquerors of the seventh and eighth centuries A.D. Arabic language and culture had an even greater impact under the influence of the Bedouin Arabs, who arrived in greater numbers from the 11th century onward.

Written Arabic is important as the vehicle of Islam and Arab culture and as a link with other Arab countries. Three forms are used today: the classical Arabic of the Koran, Algerian dialectical Arabic, and modern literary Arabic. The Arabic of the Koran is the essential base of written Arabic and the model of linguistic perfection, according to the beliefs of Islam. It is the vehicle of a vast religious, scientific, historical, and literary heritage. Arabic scholars or individuals with a good education from any country can converse with one another using classical Arabic.

In classical Arabic, only the consonants are written; vowel signs and other marks to aid in pronunciation are employed occasionally in printed texts. The script is cursive, lending itself to use as decoration, and Arabic calligraphy is an important art form. It is written from right to left.

Literary Arabic, a simplified version of classical Arabic, is used in literature, the theater, newspapers, radio, and public speaking throughout the Middle East. A majority of Algerians, however, speak only dialectical Arabic. Just over one-half of Algerians are literate, and many of these read only French.

Tamazight (the Berber language), like Arabic, is an Afro-Asiatic language, dialects of which are found throughout the Maghrib. It is primarily a spoken language, although an ancient Berber script called *tifinagh* survives among the Tuareg of the Algerian Sahara, where the characters are used more for special purposes than for communication.

There has been considerable borrowing of words between Tamazight and Arabic. In some Arabic-speaking zones the names for various flora and fauna and many places are still in Tamazight.

Several Berber dialect groups are recognizable in modern Algeria, but only the dialects of the Kabyle and Shawiya are spoken by any considerable number. The dialect of the Shawiya, which is distinguishable from but related to the Kabyle dialect, bears the mark and influence of Arabic. Separate dialects are spoken by the Tuareg and the M'zabite.

Teaching Arabic in the schools in the early years of independence.

ARABIZATION

The French attempted to "civilize" Algeria by imposing French language and culture on it. As a result, education was oriented toward French, and advanced education in classical Arabic virtually ceased except among small numbers of religious scholars. Dialectical Arabic remained the language of everyday discourse for the vast majority of the population, but it was cut off from modern intellectual and technological developments and consequently failed to develop the flexibility and vocabulary needed for modern bureaucratic, financial, and intellectual affairs.

In reaction, the leaders of the revolution and successive governments committed themselves to Arabic as the national language. The aim was to recover the precolonial past and to use it together with Arabic to restore—if not to create—a national identity. The goal of "Arabization" is a country with its own language (Arabic), religion (Islam), and national identity (Algerian) free of French language and influence.

Beginning in the late 1960s, the government of President Houari Boumedienne decreed the first steps to promote literary Arabic in the bureaucracy and in the schools. The problems inherent in this process of language planning immediately came to the fore. One of the most obvious involved literary Arabic, which for the overwhelming majority of Algerians was quite foreign. There was also an almost total lack of qualified Arabic teachers. Other obstacles included widespread use of French in the state-run media and the continued preference for French as the working language of government and of urban society. It soon became obvious to students that their prospects for gainful employment were bleak without facility in French, a fact that contributed to general public skepticism.

There has been opposition to Arabization from the Berbers. Young Kabyle students were particularly vocal in expressing their opposition. In the early 1980s their movement and demands formed the basis of the so-called Berber Question or the Kabyle "cultural movement."

Kabyle militants of the 1980s vigorously opposed Arabization of the educational system and the government bureaucracy and the adoption of literary Arabic as Algeria's official language. They demanded recognition of Tamazight as a primary national language, respect for Berber culture, and greater attention to the economic development of Kabylia and other Berber homelands. The banner on the right depicts *tifinagh*, an ancient Berber script.

THE RISKY PROFESSION OF JOURNALISM

On October 18, 1993, Smail Yefseh, a television journalist, was stabbed twice in the back and then shot in the chest and stomach. It was 8:00 in the morning and dozens of passersby watched as three well-dressed young men fatally assaulted Yefseh.

Yefseh was the seventh of over 50 Algerian journalists assassinated since 1992. Many had their throats slashed or were shot at close range in front of their families.

Some 50,000 Algerians have died in the civil war that started when the country's first free parliamentary elections were nullified in January 1992. According to statistics released by security forces, 6,388 Algerians were killed in 1994. Government figures show that other professions have suffered greater losses than the press—682 civil servants, 350 merchants, 304 peasants, 122 veterans of the war of independence, and 101 teachers were murdered in 1995, compared to 21 journalists. But the latter represent a high proportion of the approximately 500 journalists working in Algeria. And the killing of journalists symbolizes the freedom of speech lost by all Algerians because of the war.

The fundamentalists do not have access to the established, legal media. The clandestine fundamentalist radio and TV stations broadcast

NAMES

For those familiar with the European tradition of using just a forename, optional middle name, and surname, names in the Arab world can seem perplexing, not least because they can run to enormous length. However, there is a logical structure to the Arab naming convention that, once seen, makes it simple to decipher a person's recent ancestry.

Suppose a man's name is Ali bin Ahmed bin Saleh Al-Fulani. He is called Ali by his friends and family. His family name is Al-Fulani. *Bin* means "son of," so bin Ahmed bin Saleh means that he is the son of Ahmed who is in turn the son of Saleh. Many Arabs can give their paternal ancestors' names for at least five or six generations, and often many more.

What about women's names? Ali's sister is named Nura bint Ahmed bin Saleh Al-Fulani. *Bint* means "daughter of." Thus her name means Nura, the daughter of Ahmed who is the son of Saleh. So we have her given name, her father's name, her grandfather's name, and the family name.

It is interesting to note that when an Arab woman marries, she does not change her name. When the above-mentioned Nura marries, her name remains exactly the same. Her children, however, take their father's name.

Arab personal names are particularly confusing to the Western reader. Arab names include paternal genealogy and sometimes also indicate family name, tribal affiliation, and village or region of origin. For example, a man named Abd al Rahman ibn (or ben) Qasim ibn Mohammed (or Mohamed) El (or Al) Bayadh would be recognized as the son of Qasim, the grandson of Mohammed, and a native of the town of El Bayadh. The man would be addressed as Mister (or his title, if any) Abd al Rahman; in spoken Arabic, names are elided, so that in this instance the name would be pronounced as if it were spelled Abdur Rahman. In many instances the Western press spells such names as Abdel (or Abdul) Rahman, implying incorrectly that the man's first name is Abdel and his last name Rahman. Many Arabic names, such as the one in this example, are designations of the attributes of God (Allah). *Abd al* means "servant of," and *Rahman* means "merciful"; thus the name literally means "the servant of the Merciful (God)."

All newspapers, book publishing, and broadcasting activities are under the control of the central government.
The main Arabic language daily is called El Massaa.
The main French language daily is El Moudjahid.
There are no English language newspapers published in the country, although the French newspaper Horizons 2000 *prints one page in English.*

sporadically. Underground papers circulate in small numbers. To transmit a pro-Islamic Salvation Front (FIS) broadcast or print pro-FIS literature is to court death—in much the same way that journalists risk their lives going to work.

Opposite: **French language newspapers in Algeria.**

ARTS

AFTER INDEPENDENCE from French rule, the government placed great emphasis on restoring Algeria's national, especially Arab, heritage. Each administration called for a revival of the art forms that had disappeared during the colonial period. Funds were allocated to restore historic monuments and archaeological sites, and to create libraries and museums that recounted Algerian history.

The government also opened handicraft centers around the country to encourage the ancient crafts of rug-making, pottery, embroidery, jewelry-making, and brass work. The National Institute of Music reintroduced traditional music, dance and folklore originating from ancient Arabia and Moorish Spain.

Throughout the struggle for independence and during the current civil war, many Algerian artists, including moviemakers, writers, and actors, have been killed for being politically outspoken.

Above: **Hand of Fatima, a traditional Arab jewelry design believed to bring good luck.**

Left: **Woven rugs hanging in a market.**

Opposite: **Pottery is a traditional Algerian handicraft.**

A musician plays the *ghita*, a traditional instrument of Algeria.

RAI MUSIC

Rai began as tribal music in the countryside around Oran, a seacoast city with notoriously uninhibited traditions that has been a meeting place for various musical traditions, including Arab, French, Spanish, and African. Gnaoul rhythms, accompanied on rosewood flutes and rudimentary tambourines, created a kind of urban music. "Ha-rai," a sort of ancestor of the modern "oh yeah," was the music's omnipresent refrain, so it became known as Rai.

In the beginning, Rai was mainly performed at traditional festivals and weddings. Due to urbanization in the early 20th century some people from Relizane (east of Oran) migrated to Oran, where they performed for weddings, parties, and at bars and lounges.

The music then began to evolve into what is now recognizable as Rai—a blend of Berber, Moroccan, Spanish, and French music. The format of Rai comes from *meddahas*, female poets and singers who sang Arabic love poetry. The female singers of the 1920s and 1930s sang in deep voices and were accompanied by rosewood flutes and various percussion instruments.

In the 1950s, a lot of horn instruments were added, as well as the accordion and some violin—and modern Rai was born. Big names of the 1950s and 1960s were Cheikh Boualem, Belabbas, Hourari, and Bellemou Messaoud. This modern Rai was influenced by jazz and cha-cha.

By the late 1970s some producers started "pop Rai," which uses synthesizers to duplicate the original sounds. Pop Rai explicitly protested against the powerlessness young people felt, and less explicitly, against political inertia and social inflexibility in Algeria. Modern Rai emphasizes strong pleasures and the inevitable pains of existence: the joy of sex, the pain of love, food, alcohol, unemployment, and the daily grind.

Besides having made Rai the other Algerian export besides oil, new stars such as Cheb Khaled have rapidly transformed their music into a vehicle of youthful rebellion. That has put them on a collision course with Islamic extremism. The austere Islamic-socialist state condemned Rai for its lascivious rhythms and often licentious lyrics but allowed it to function underground as a sort of pressure-release valve.

Until the 1980s, little or nothing was known of Rai outside Algeria, partly because the music was mostly on cassette tapes of anything but professional standards. Rai crossed over to France in the mid-1980s and then went global.

Ferhat, a popular Berber singer and activist.

RAI MUSICIANS UNDER ATTACK

Rai music is accused of spreading corrupt Western values among the young (who in Algeria represent a good 75 percent of the population). Thus, in recent months, more or less all Rai stars have been condemned to death by Islamic fundamentalists. Some militant religious leaders just called for a *fatwa*, an order to all Muslims to kill a particular person, on singers they disliked. "What the terrorists want to show," said Cheb Khaled, the recognized king of Rai, "is that you can continue to sing Rai only abroad or in hiding. … You can expect only the worst from people who fight to spread their own unhappiness to everyone." Cheb Khaled has not been able to live in Algeria in recent years. He currently lives in Paris.

97

Assia Djebar is the author of novels, such as *Femmes d'Alger dans leur appartment* (*Women of Algiers in their Apartment*, 1980), which paint the moral dilemmas of families in the midst of social change.

LITERATURE

While under French rule, many Algerian-born French writers flourished in Algeria, of which the most famous is Albert Camus.

From 1920, when the first Algerian novel was published (*Ahmed Ben Mostapha, goumier* by Ben Chérif), until 1950, literature tended to copy French models.

Around 1950 to 1956, a change took place in the literature, which began an interrogation on Algerian identity and the place of the writer in Algeria. Writers like Mouloud Feraoun, Mohammed Dib, Mouloud Mammeri, and Malek Ouary began to proclaim their difference from French culture.

The war of independence produced a literature of combat, evident in the work of Kateb Yacine, Malek Haddad, Mouloud Mammeri, and Mohammed Dib. Malek Haddad's *Le Malheur en danger* (*Distress in Danger*) started an interest in poetry. Assia Djebar became known for her novels highlighting the situation of women. Journals were also an important part of linguistic production during this period, especially those of Djamal Amrani, Mouloud Feraoun, and Ahmed Taleb Ibrahimi.

After the war of independence, another period began, characterized by a questioning of earlier themes. Mohammed Dib's work became quite personal and modernist. Kateb Yacine produced plays in Arabic. Nabile Farès pleaded for pluralism and openness, followed by Ali Bouhmadi and Mouloud Achour. The poetry of Noureddine Aba, Hamid Tibouchi, Tahar Djaout, and Malek Alloula is of particular interest.

ALBERT CAMUS

Albert Camus, born in Mondovi (modern Drean), Algeria, on November 7, 1913, earned a worldwide reputation as a novelist and essayist and won the Nobel Prize for literature in 1957. Born in extreme poverty, Camus attended lycée and university in Algiers, where he developed an abiding interest in sports and the theater. In 1938 he became a journalist with *Alger-Republicain*, an anticolonialist newspaper. While working for this daily he wrote detailed reports on the condition of poor Arabs in the Kabyle region.

Through his writings, and in some measure against his will, Camus became the leading moral voice of his generation during the 1950s.

During the war Camus published the main works associated with his doctrine of the absurd—his view that human life is rendered ultimately meaningless by the fact of death and that the individual cannot make rational sense of his experience. These works include the novel *The Stranger* (1942), perhaps his finest work of fiction, and *The Myth of Sisyphus* (1942).

From this point on, Camus was concerned mainly with exploring avenues of rebellion against the absurd as he strove to create something like a humane stoicism. *The Plague* (1947) is a symbolic novel in which the important achievement of those who fight bubonic plague in Oran lies not in the little success they have but in their assertion of human dignity and endurance. In the controversial essay *The Rebel* (1951), he argued in favor of Mediterranean humanism, advocating nature and moderation rather than historicism and violence. Camus died in an automobile accident near Sens, France in 1960, at the height of his fame.

LITERATURE'S LOSSES

Recently, many writers have died because of their criticism of FIS militants. One casualty of this literary hit list, which includes poet Youcef Sebti, was Rachid Mimouni, who died in January 1995 of hepatitis contracted in Morocco where he lived following threats by fundamentalists in Algeria. Mimouni's novel *The Curse,* winner of the Prix du Levant award, focuses on political events in Algeria in the last few years. Women, a chief concern of FIS militants, are at the center of his novel. As one of his characters says, "They need an enemy, a great Satan who can crystallise the causes of all evil. And, well, the Jews have served that purpose already." His women characters drink, smoke, swear; by contrast, the only veiled woman in the novel, an FIS militant, is ridiculed, as is Algeria's military government.

Rachid Mimouni. Despite death threats and the Algerian government's refusal to provide protection for any intellectual, Mimouni continued to write.

Another casualty is novelist Tahar Djaout, killed in 1993. Djaout was considered to be the heir of the writers of the "1952 Generation": Mohammed Dib, Mouloud Mammeri, Mouloud Feraoun, and Kateb Yacine. A native of Azzefoun, Kabylia, Djaout moved to Algiers to complete his education. In 1974, he became a journalist first with *El Moudjahid* and then with *Algérie-Actualité.* In 1993, he founded the weekly *Ruptures* with friends and was its chief editor until his death. Influenced by the ethnological writings of Mouloud Feraoun and the poetic writings of Kateb Yacine, Tahar Djaout explored the past and the present, incorporating the history of North Africa, the colonization of Algeria, and his childhood experience in Kabylia. His last three novels described aspects of a search for an identity illustrated by the narrators' journeys in space and time.

Djaout strongly disapproved of the government's control of public life. In *Les Chercheurs d'Os* (*Searchers for Bones*), set in the aftermath of the war of independence, the plot revolves around the retrieval of the remains of Algerian combatants for reburial. The quest for his older brother's remains requires a young villager to undertake his first journey outside his home. Upon his return with his brother's remains, the young man questions the purpose of the quest for bones, suggesting that the villagers, in fact, fear the combatants' ghosts and that an official and deeper burial of the bones would offer more reassurance. He realizes that the villagers are more dead than the combatants whose remains are being reburied.

Les Vigiles (*The Vigils*) reflects the corrosive nature of Algerian society during the reign of the FLN government. The story is about a young Algerian teacher who has developed a novel and efficient weaving loom. He wishes to register and patent his invention, but he is hampered by a number of inextricable bureaucratic difficulties.

Tahar Djaout, killed at age 39, was another great loss to Algerian letters.

Director Belkacem Hadjaj is one of several important Algerian filmmakers.

CINEMA

The Algerian art form that has earned the greatest acclaim in Algeria and worldwide is the cinema. Most Algerian movies are produced by the National Film Company, ONAPROC. Algerians have won several international film festival awards for dramas and documentaries about colonialism, revolution, and controversial social topics. Mohamed Lakhdar Hamina won the 1982 Cannes Film Festival award for *Desert Wind,* about the difficult lives Algerian women confront in a traditional society.

Director Belkacem Hadjaj's *The Drop* (1982/1989) presents an eerie look at the plight of rural migrants who work on housing in which they cannot afford to live. To a jarring score of grinding tractor gears and hammering, the migrants are shown as milked by the city; at the end of the day, even their sweat is symbolically collected, drop by drop, in an urn.

Mohamed Rachid Benhadj's *Desert Rose* (1989) tells the intimate, yet unsentimental, story of Mousa, a severely handicapped young man who fights to overcome his infirmities in his search for love and a place in society in a remote oasis village.

Director Hafsa Zinai Koudil, a tense, chain-smoking woman, got her idea for a movie from a true story reported in 1990. A man had his wife beaten up by exorcists because she refused to wear the veil. Her attackers were brought to justice but only given token sentences.

The Devil in the Feminine Case describes an urban couple whose eldest son is won over to the cause of Islamic fundamentalism. His father also espouses the cause. The two become obsessed with the idea of getting the mother to wear the veil. When she refuses, they declare that she is possessed by the devil and hire three men to exorcise her. The torture session ends with the woman rushed to the hospital. She is handicapped for life, and her husband goes out of his mind.

"I made the film in an atmosphere of terror," says Hafsa. They had no police protection, and throughout the filming crew members took turns to look out for signs of trouble. The film was not distributed in Algeria. *The Devil in the Feminine Case* has been shown, however, at the 1994 Amiens Festival and at the 1995 International Women's Film Festival.

Hafsa is also the author of four novels, starting with the autobiographical *The End of a Dream* in 1984. Her latest novel, *The Discomposed Past*, published in 1992, denounces the status of women in Algeria.

Merzak Allouache's *Bab El-Oued City* depicts the dangers inherent in the recent rise of Islamic fundamentalism in Algeria. Bab El-Oued is a working class district of Algiers. One morning shortly after the bloody riots of October 1988, Boualem, a young worker in a bakery who works at night and sleeps during the day, commits an act that puts the entire district in turmoil. Unable to stand the noise from one of the many rooftop loudspeakers broadcasting the propaganda of a fundamentalist group, he rips the speaker out and throws it away. The extremists, led by Said, regard the removal of the speaker as provocative and want to make an example of him. Violence escalates when Said's younger sister is caught meeting Boualem, with whom she is secretly in love.

Bab El-Oued City has attracted considerable attention, winning both an International Film Critics prize and a Prix Gervais at the Cannes Film Festival (1994). While shooting *Bab El-Oued City*, violence fully erupted in Algeria. Allouache shot some of the exterior scenes with a camera hidden under his coat. He lives in Paris and is working on a sequel to be shot in an Algerian section of Paris.

LEISURE

ALGERIAN SOCIAL LIFE revolves around visiting family. Relatives call on each other frequently to share sweet treats and lengthy conversation. Outsiders are rarely invited, but when they are, they are treated with great hospitality and generosity. Hospitality is an important tradition for all Arabs as well as Berbers. A traditional Berber saying expresses the Algerian emphasis on hospitality: "When you come to our house, it is we who are your guests, for this is your home."

Similar to other Mediterranean peoples, Algerians like to go to beaches. The Algerian middle class enjoys summer resorts along the coast. Here families swim, water-ski, play tennis, and fish at modern facilities. Most families vacation in August, which is when most Algerians who work in Europe return home.

Soccer is the most popular national sport. People of all ages play and watch soccer matches. Young boys can be seen kicking balls outside city housing projects. In rural areas, boys must tend their sheep rather than play.

Girls are less visible at play. They are expected to help their mothers. Some jump rope and play a version of the Western string game between two people.

As children get older, girls are seen less, and boys take to city streets. Young men, especially the unemployed, hang around street corners and cafés looking for activity. Despite the size of some cities, there is very little to do outside of home, school, and work.

Above: **Men converse in a park. Women spend less time in public.**

Opposite: **Playing checkers is a popular pastime.**

Above: **Men spend many leisure hours in outdoor cafés.**

Opposite: **Playing soccer is a favorite pastime with boys.**

LEISURELY PURSUITS

Life moves at a leisurely pace in Algeria. Algerians do not rush around frantically trying to do a million things. Most leisure activities in Algeria are family oriented.

Algerians enjoy eating well, but do not eat out often. Most Algerians savor eating good traditional food at home in the company of friends and extended family. They welcome any excuse for a banquet. Women, especially, enjoy these get-togethers, because it is generally the only leisure activity they can safely participate in given the militant FIS campaign of terror against women.

Men, however, are less restricted in their movement, and tend to congregate in cafés to discuss local affairs and events and to exchange gossip over coffee, mint tea, or a refreshing sharbat.

A DIFFICULT TIME FOR WOMEN IN SPORTS

In 1991, Hassiba Boulmerka became the first African woman to win a gold medal at the World Track and Field Championships when she won the 1,500 meters. A year later in Barcelona, she became Algeria's first Olympic champion, winning the 1,500 in 3 minutes 55.30 seconds.

Whether her achievements instill pride or fury in her countrymen depends, she says, on whom one asks. "In general, I get positive reactions in Algeria because I'm a symbol of my country. But like every symbol, there are some who like me and some who don't." Every time she runs in shorts, she incurs the wrath of Muslim fundamentalists, who have spat on her, pelted her with rocks, and called her blasphemous for "running with naked legs in front of thousands of men."

Although she lives abroad nine months out of the year, she returns to try to be a role model for Algerian girls. Some school sports programs similar to the one that spawned her career have been discontinued. "The situation is difficult in Algeria, especially for women," she says. "But it's important to have courage and set an example by training there, so I do. It'll never be easy for women in Algeria. But my gold medal wasn't simply a victory for the moment. It was a victory for the future. It gave a glimpse of what women could do in Algeria."

FESTIVALS

ALGERIA'S MAJOR RELIGIOUS holidays, including Eid al-Fitr, Eid al-Adha, Muharram, and Mawlid an-Nabi, have long histories going back to the time of the founding of Islam. They fall on different dates each year because they are linked to the Muslim calendar rather than the Gregorian calendar. The Gregorian calendar is solar, while the Muslim calendar is lunar, and therefore the Muslim year is 11 days shorter than the Gregorian year.

Above: **The opening ceremony of the Horse Festival in Tiaret.**

Opposite: **A festival in Timgad draws a large crowd.**

PUBLIC HOLIDAYS

New Year's Day: January 1

Labor Day: May 1

Commemoration Day: June 19

Independence Day: July 5

Anniversary of the Revolution: November 1

Ramadan: variable

Eid al-Fitr: variable

Eid al-Adha: variable

Hijriyya calendar New Year: variable

Mawlid an-Nabi (Prophet Mohammed's birthday): variable

OTHER HOLIDAYS

Leilat al-Meiraj (ascension of Prophet Mohammed): variable

Muharram (Islamic New Year's Day): variable

Ashoura: variable

EID AL-ADHA

Also called Eid al-Kebir, or the Major Festival, Eid al-Adha is celebrated on the 10th of Dhu al-Hijja, the last month of the year. Although Muslims observe this holiday in their hometowns all around the world, its most sacred observance is in Mina, a small village four miles (6.4 km) east of Mecca. There hundreds of thousands of Muslims observe the sacrifice as part of the pilgrimage to Mecca and to other sacred sites nearby—the Hajj.

The teachings of the Prophet decree that heads of families who are able to do so must purchase a sheep for sacrifice. The meat of the slaughtered animal is shared with the poor; the Prophet recommended giving one-third to the poor, one-third to neighbors and friends, and letting one-third remain in the family. The sacrifice signifies the willingness of Ibrahim (known to Christians as Abraham) to sacrifice what was most precious to him, his son. The sacrificer symbolically affirms that he or she is willing to give up, for the sake of God, that which is dearest to him or her. It is a sacred gesture of thanksgiving and a measure of charity.

Like Eid al-Fitr, Eid al-Adha is traditionally a family gathering. For pilgrims camped at Mina, it also marks the end of their pilgrimage and a return to normal life.

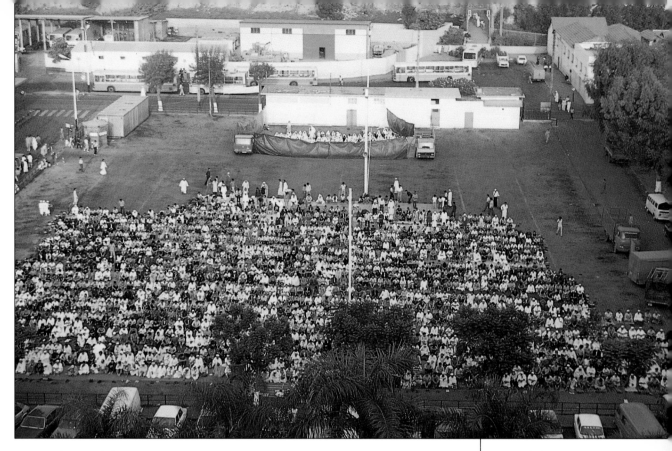

EID AL-FITR

Also called the Eid as-Sagheer, or the Minor Festival, this holiday occurs on the first day of the month of Shawwal, immediately after Ramadan, the fasting month. Eid al-Fitr begins in the morning with the men going to the mosque for the morning prayer. This is followed, according to the teachings of the Prophet, by a visit to the cemetery.

These solemn religious expressions then change into a happy festival in the homes of heads of families. Gifts and money are given to children and to newly married daughters. More significant is the joyous return for all to a normal life. Islamic law requires that *zakat al-fitr,* or the alms of breaking off the fast, be given to the poor.

This festival brings Algeria to a standstill for at least two days, although feasting and festivities often continue for up to a week. People in Algeria prepare by scrubbing their houses and painting the shutters. Special food is prepared well in advance and new clothes are bought for the occasion. On the holiday, everyone dresses up in their best clothes and brings pastries to their friends and relatives.

Above: **Celebrants for the Eid prayer overflow Algiers Mosque.**

Opposite: **The sacrifice of a sheep is traditional for Eid al-Adha.**

Festival celebrants in southern Algeria.

MAWLID AN-NABI

Prophet Mohammed's birthday is celebrated on the 12th day of the third Islamic month, Rebbi ul-awal. During the first two centuries of Islam, this festival was not observed. For one thing, the exact date of Mohammed's birth was not known. By the ninth century a set body of traditions about the teachings of the Prophet had become standardized. One precedent in the Prophet's life that emerged was that many important events had occurred on Mondays. His hegira to Medina and his death were thought by many to have occurred on Monday. Tradition formed in favor of Monday, the 12th day of Rebbi ul-awal, as the anniversary of his birth.

Mawlid an-Nabi has become a major religious festival for Muslims in the Islamic world, and Algeria is no exception. This day is observed with special prayers. Men congregate at the local mosque or make a special journey to the main mosque to hear the imam tell the story of Mohammed's life. Women gather in each other's homes for prayers.

HORSE AND CAMEL FESTIVALS

Many cities celebrate traditional horse and camel festivals. Two of the better known are the Horse Festival of Tiaret and the Camel Festival, or simply the Metlili Festival, celebrated in Metlili near Ghardaia.

During the Horse Festival, there are horse races and parades, where riders from other regions are represented. There is also a competition called fantasia, in which the riders must aim and shoot at a target while their horses are in full gallop, and then bring their horses to an abrupt stop.

The Camel Festival at Metlili lasts two full days in March. There is a fantasia at this one too. Another popular event is the camel dancing, where the camel riders make their camels dance to the accompaniment of traditional instruments. For a percussion effect, the riders shoot their rifles into the ground, which makes the ground vibrate under the spectators' feet. There is also a bride parade, a traditional custom that goes back to ancient times.

A camel race draws a large crowd of spectators. Families from the surrounding areas come by the truckload or in caravan to attend.

113

FOOD

TRADITIONAL ALGERIAN CUISINE is rich in variety and delights the senses with special seasonings. Coriander is the chief flavoring throughout the Maghrib region. In Algeria, chefs also include ginger, hot peppers, pimiento, cumin, mint, cinnamon, onions, garlic, cloves, and parsley.

The agricultural areas of Algeria specialize in lemons, olives, tomatoes, peppers, dates, grapes, potatoes, almonds, and figs. Fish and other seafood are available along the coast. Chickens, sheep, goats, cattle, and horses are raised by nomadic peoples. No pork is served.

Algerian cuisine and cooking methods reflect the mix of cultures. The Berbers traditionally cooked stews of lamb, poultry, and vegetables. The Arabs introduced spices and mouthwatering pastries. The French chiefly contributed their incomparable breads, and some Spanish influence can be seen in the use of olives and olive oil.

Opposite: **An open-air market displays the wealth of produce available in Algeria.**

Left: **Tea and snacks are an Algerian specialty.**

A plate of couscous ready to eat.

COUSCOUS

Couscous is often, but incorrectly, described as a grain. Actually, it's a type of pasta made from a dough that contains durum wheat (semolina) and water. Instead of being rolled out or extruded to form noodles, the dough is rubbed through a sieve to make tiny pellets. Cooking experts believe the word "couscous" is onomatopoeic for the sound of the pellets hitting the water.

But couscous also refers to a North African style of eating. The couscous arrives in a steaming mound on a platter. A spicy stew is ladled over the couscous, followed by a spoonful of *harissa* (fiery hot sauce). Often, for extra flavor, the couscous is steamed over the stew. Like pasta, couscous can accommodate an almost endless variety of toppings and sauces.

Couscous is a staple throughout North Africa, where it is believed to have been eaten since Roman times. Moroccan couscous is the mildest, lightest and fluffiest, while Algerian couscous is firm and dense. Couscous also turns up in Sicily, where it is served with seafood, and in Tunisia, where one version calls for pomegranates and orange flower water and is served as a dessert.

Couscous is probably Algeria's most popular dish, and is often called its national dish. It is usually served surrounded with lamb or chicken in a bed of cooked vegetables and covered with gravy. Often, onions, turnips, raisins, garbanzo beans, and red bell peppers are added. Couscous mixed with honey, cinnamon, and almonds makes a dessert that tastes similar to rice pudding.

ALGERIAN COUSCOUS CHICKEN STEW

Couscous refers both to the prepared grain itself and to stews made with couscous. The Mediterranean and Middle Eastern countries each have their own preferences and recipes for making couscous. In Algeria, meat is fried in olive oil first, and tomatoes are rarely omitted. A fiery condiment made with hot pimentos, called *harissa*, is always served with Algerian couscous and is enjoyed by those who are accustomed to hot foods. In Algeria stews are simmered slowly for several hours until everything in the pot is blended together and the meat falls off the bones.

Serves 6

2 to 4 tablespoons olive oil
2 to 3 pounds (1–1.3 kg) chicken, cut into serving-size pieces
3 cups chicken broth, homemade or canned
3 carrots, cut in about 2-inch (5 cm) chunks
2 onions, coarsely chopped
2 turnips, cut in about 2-inch (5 cm) chunks
3 cloves garlic, finely chopped, or 1 teaspoon garlic granules
2 teaspoons ground coriander
$^1/_4$ teaspoon each ground red pepper and ground turmeric
3 zucchini, cut into $^1/_4$-inch (0.5 cm) slices
2 cups cooked garbanzo beans
4 to 6 cups cooked couscous (cook according to directions on package and keep warm)

1. Heat 2 tablespoons oil in saucepan or Dutch oven over medium-high heat. Add chicken pieces and fry until brown (add more oil if necessary to prevent sticking), about 6 to 10 minutes per side. Remove from pan and set aside. Fry in batches if necessary.

2. Add chicken broth, carrots, onions, turnips, garlic, coriander, red pepper, and turmeric in the same pan, mix well, and bring to a boil over high heat. Reduce heat to simmer and layer zucchini, beans, and chicken on top. Cover and cook very slowly for about one hour, until chicken is very tender.

3. Mound the couscous in the middle of a platter and place chicken pieces and vegetables around it. To serve Algerian-style, place the platter in the middle of the table. The guests are given a damp towel to wipe their hands. The head of the house and then special guests are first to eat. They dip the fingers of the right hand in the platter of couscous. They then proceed to take a handful and roll it into a ball (using only the right hand). They eat it off their fingers. The chicken and stew are eaten in the same fashion.

A street vendor sells bread in Algiers.

BREAD

Bread is a staple of the Algerian diet. For many poor people, bread teamed with a few olives or dates, or perhaps with a small piece of goat cheese, is a meal in itself. This is usually accompanied by a glass of hot mint tea.

Bread, usually French loaf, is eaten at every meal. In addition to being an accompaniment to whatever food is being served, crusty chunks are useful for scooping up meat and vegetables, and for soaking up the spicy gravy that usually flavors Algerian stews. Berbers eat traditional flat cakes of mixed grains, while bread is also a traditional part of the Arab diet.

Wheat is the basis of the Algerian diet, whether it is in the form of bread or couscous. Many sayings highlight the importance of bread in traditional Algerian society.

LAMB

Lamb is one of the mainstays of Algerian cuisine. It is eaten grilled, minced
for use as a vegetable stuffing, or as a main ingredient in stews and
couscous.

A favorite lamb dish is *mechoui,* which is charcoal roasted whole lamb.
Mechoui is a favorite dish for large gatherings and picnics. A Berber
specialty, mechoui is prepared by rubbing the lamb with garlic and spices.
The lamb is then roasted over an open-air spit at the beach or in the village
or garden. It is basted regularly with herbed butter so that it becomes crispy
on the outside and soft and tender on the inside. The best mechoui is so
tender that the crisp skin peels away easily, and the meat comes away in
the hand. Guests pluck bits of lamb from the roast to eat with bread, usually
French bread.

FIGS

Figs comprise a large genus, Ficus, of deciduous and evergreen tropical and subtropical trees, shrubs, and vines belonging to the mulberry family. Commercially, the most important fig is *Ficus carica*, the tree that produces the edible fig fruit. Among the most ancient cultivated fruit trees, the fig is indigenous to the eastern Mediterranean and the southwest region of Asia where its cultivation probably began. It is now grown in warm, semiarid areas throughout the world.

The fruit-bearing fig ranges from a bushlike 3 feet (1 m) to a moderately tall tree that may grow up to 39 feet (12 m) in height. It is characterized by its dark green, deeply lobed leaves.

The fig bears no visible flowers; its flowers are borne within a round, fleshy structure, the syconium, which matures into the edible fig. The common fig bears only female flowers, but develops its fruits without pollination. Varieties of the Smyrna type also bear only female flowers, but in order to produce fruit, they must be pollinated artificially.

Fig trees are propagated through rooted cuttings taken from the wood of older trees. They grow best in moderately dry areas that have no rain during the period of fruit maturation; during this period, humidity might hinder the process of fruit drying, much of which occurs on the tree. The partially dried fruit drops to the ground, where it is gathered and the drying process completed. Some fruit may be picked from the tree before it dries, and eaten as fresh fruit.

MEDITERRANEAN SPECIALTIES

Algeria shares most of its culinary mainstays with the other countries of the Mediterranean region. Dishes such as tabouleh and hummus are found throughout the Mediterranean, especially in the Middle East, although the spicing may vary somewhat. For instance, Middle Eastern tabouleh uses more lemon and less oil than that prepared in Algeria. Chickpeas, sesame paste, olives, dates, and lemons are common ingredients in Algerian cooking. Desserts like baklava, usually associated with Greek cooking, are also found in Algeria. Mint tea is a favorite throughout the region.

DRINKS

The most popular drink in North Africa is mint-flavored tea. Algeria is no exception. However, mint tea is not the only drink in town. Fruit drink stands abound, piled high with fruits in season and tempting glasses of juice on display. Orange juice, sugar-cane juice, and lemon juice are popular. Drinks based on citrus fruits, pomegranates, and grapes are also favorites. Children are usually offered a glass of sweet apricot juice.

Also popular are sharbats, which are fruit- or nut-flavored milk drinks poured over shaved ice. Refreshing yogurt-based drinks flavored with fruit or nuts are also found at these drink stands.

Algerians are also fond of coffee, and drink it in various forms. Most common is thick black coffee, but coffee is also served half and half—half coffee and half hot milk. Coffee is also served spiced, usually with cloves, cinnamon, or cardamon. Ras el Hanout is an ancient coffee drink mixed with anywhere from 10 to 26 spices.

A traditional Berber drink is made from goat cheese. The cheese is crumbled and crushed with dates and well water. This drink is almost a complete meal in itself and is most often drunk by nomadic goat herders.

Mint tea is the favorite Algerian drink, and it is the standard offering to a visitor. Street stands selling mint tea are ubiquitous.

121

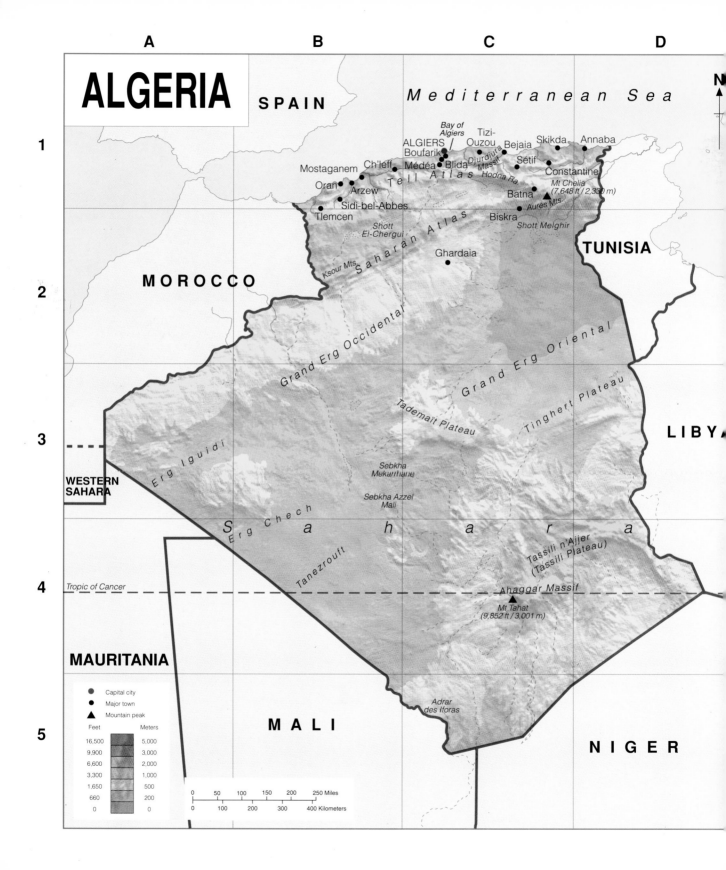

ALGERIA

A   **B**   **C**   **D**

N

Mediterranean Sea

SPAIN

1

Bay of
Algiers
ALGIERS
Boufarik
Tizi-
Ouzou
Bejaia
Skikda
Annaba
Mostaganem
Ch'leff
Médéa
Blida
Djurdjura
Massif
Sétif
Constantine
Oran
Arzew
Tell Atlas
Hodna Ra.
Mt Chelia
(7,648 ft / 2,330 m)
Sidi-bel-Abbes
Batna
Tlemcen
Aures Mts.
Biskra

MOROCCO
Shott
El-Chergui
Shott Melghir

TUNISIA

2

Ksour Mts
Saharan Atlas
Ghardaia

Grand Erg Occidental
Grand Erg Oriental

LIBYA

Tademaït Plateau
Tinghert Plateau

3

WESTERN
SAHARA

Erg Iguidi
Sebkha
Mekarrhane

Sebkha Azzel
Mali

S   *a*   *h*   *a*   *r*   *a*
Erg Chech

Tassili n'Ajjer
(Tassili Plateau)

Tanezrouft

4

Tropic of Cancer
Ahaggar Massif
Mt Tahat
(9,852 ft / 3,001 m)

MAURITANIA

Adrar
des Iforas

5

MALI

NIGER

Capital city
Major town
Mountain peak

Feet	Meters
16,500	5,000
9,900	3,000
6,600	2,000
3,300	1,000
1,650	500
660	200
0	0

0   50   100   150   200   250 Miles

0   100   200   300   400 Kilometers

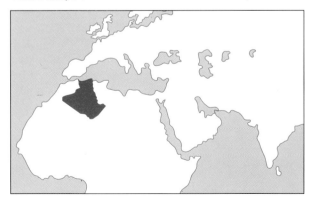

QUICK NOTES

OFFICIAL NAME
Conventional long form: Democratic and Popular Republic of Algeria
Conventional short form: Algeria
Local long form: Al Jumhuriyah al Jaza'iriyah ad Demuqratiyah ash Shabiyah
Local short form: Al Jaza'ir

CAPITAL
Algiers

MAJOR CITIES
Oran, Constantine

AREA
919,595 square miles (2,381,740 square km)

HIGHEST POINT
Mt. Tahat, 9,852 feet (3,001 m)

POPULATION
28,539,321 (July 1995 estimate)

ADMINISTRATIVE DIVISIONS
Adrar, Ain Defla, Ain Temouchent, Alger, Annaba, Batna, Bechar, Bejaia, Biskra, Blida, Bordj Bou Arreridj, Bouira, Boumerdes, Chief, Constantine, Djelfa, El Bayadh, El Oued, El Tarf, Ghardaia, Guelma, Illizi, Jijel, Khenchela, Laghouat, Mascara, Médéa, Mila, Mostaganem, M'Sila, Naama, Oran, Ouargla, Oum el Bouaghi, Relizane, Saida, Sétif, Sidi-bel-Abbes, Skikda, Souk Ahras, Tamanghasset, Tebessa, Tiaret, Tindouf, Tipaza, Tissemsilt, Tizi-Ouzou, Tlemcen

MAJOR LANGUAGES
Arabic (official), French, Berber dialects

FLAG
Two equal vertical bands of green (hoist side) and white with a red five-pointed star within a red crescent; the crescent, star, and color green are symbols of Islam, the state religion

CURRENCY
1 Algerian dinar (DA) = 100 centimes
55.94 dinar = US$1

IMPORTANT DATES
Independence from France: July 5, 1962
Beginning of the revolution: November 1, 1954

MAJOR RELIGIONS
Sunni Islam (state religion): 99%
Christianity and Judaism: 1%

MAJOR RELIGIOUS FESTIVALS
Eid al-Fitr
Eid al-Adha
Mawlid an-Nabi
Muharram

PRINCIPAL EXPORTS
Mineral fuels, lubricants, vegetables, tobacco, hides, dates

PRINCIPAL IMPORTS
Machinery, transport equipment, food, basic manufactures

GLOSSARY

amazigh
"Free man," a term Berbers call themselves.

ayla
A small lineage, the members of which claim descent through the male line from a common grandfather or great-grandfather.

baraka
Special blessedness or grace.

bin/bint
Part of Muslim names meaning "son of" or "daughter of."

burnous ("BUHR-noos")
Long hooded robe.

Casbah ("KAHZ-bah")
The old part of Algiers, from the Arabic word for a Turkish fortress.

colon ("koh-LOHN")
French word for colonist.

gourbi (GOHR-be")
Rural dwelling constructed of mud and branches, stone, or clay.

haik
A long piece of cloth that is draped over the body to hide the lower part of the face and cover the clothes underneath.

hajj
Pilgrimage to Mecca, required of every Muslim with adequate means.

Maghrib
Arabic for "west," the name refers to a region of northern Africa including Morocco, Algeria, Tunisia, and sometimes Libya.

marabout
Holy man.

meddahas
Female poets and singers who sang Arabic love poetry.

Rai
A popular and traditional music indigenous to Algeria.

sebkhas
Salt marshes.

shahadah
The testimony repeated by Muslims, "There is no god but God (Allah), and Mohammed is his Prophet."

shott/shatt
Shallow salt marsh.

souk
Market.

tifinagh
Ancient script used by the Tuareg. This is the only traditional writing for Berbers.

wadi ("WAH-dee")
Dry streambeds found in the Sahara that were formed during earlier wet periods.

BIBLIOGRAPHY

Ageron. *Modern Algeria: A History from Eighteen Thirty to the Present.* Lawrenceville NJ: Africa World Press, 1990.

Camus, Albert. *The Stranger.* New York NY: Vintage, 1989.

Djebar, Assia, translated by Marjolijn De Jager. *Women of Algiers in their Apartment.* Charlottesville VA: University Press of Virginia, 1992.

Lazreg, Marnia. *The Eloquence of Silence: Algerian Women in Question.* New York NY: Routledge, 1994.

Lerner Publications. *Algeria in Pictures.* Minneapolis: Minneapolis MN: Lerner Publications, 1992.

Metz, Helen Chapin. *Algeria: A Country Study.* Washington DC: Library of Congress, 1995.

Targ-Brill, Marlene. *Algeria (Enchantment of the World).* Danbury CT: Children's Press, 1990.

INDEX

INDEX

INDEX